ALBEE

in an hour

E. TERESA CHOATE

D1011922

SUSAN C. MOORE, SERIES EDITOR

PLAYWRIGHTS in an hour
know the playwright, love the play

IN AN HOUR BOOKS • HANOVER, NEW HAMPSHIRE • INANHOURBOOKS.COM
AN IMPRINT OF SMITH AND KRAUS PUBLISHERS, INC • SMITHANDKRAUS.COM

With grateful thanks to Carl R. Mueller,
whose fascinating introductions to his translations of the Greek and
German playwrights provided inspiration for this series.

Published by In an Hour Books
an imprint of Smith and Kraus, Inc.
177 Lyme Road, Hanover, NH 03755
inanhourbooks.com SmithandKraus.com

Know the playwright, love the play.

In an Hour, In a Minute, and Theater IQ are registered trademarks of
In an Hour Books.

Front cover design by Dan Mehling, dmehling@gmail.com
Text design by Kate Mueller, Electric Dragon Productions
Book production by Dede Cummings Design, DCDesign@sover.net

ISBN-13: 978-1-936232-01-7
ISBN-10: 1-936232-01-4
Library of Congress Control Number: 2009943225

CONTENTS

Why Playwrights in an Hour?

This new series by Smith and Kraus Publishers titled Playwrights in an Hour has a dual purpose for being; one academic, the other general. For the general reader, this volume, as well as the many others in the series, offers in compact form the information needed for a basic understanding and appreciation of the works of each volume's featured playwright. Which is not to say that there don't exist volumes on end devoted to each playwright under consideration. But inasmuch as few are blessed with enough time to read the splendid scholarship that is available, a brief, highly focused accounting of the playwright's life and work is in order.

The central feature of the series, a thirty- to forty-page essay, integrates the playwright into the context of his or her time and place. And the volumes, though written to high standards of academic integrity, are accessible in style and approach to the general reader as well as to the student, and of course to the theater professional and theatergoer.

These books will serve for the brushing up of one's knowledge of a playwright's career, to the benefit of theater work or theatergoing. The Playwrights in an Hour series represents all periods of Western theater: Aeschylus to Shakespeare to Wedekind to Ibsen to Williams to Beckett, and on to the great contemporary playwrights who continue to offer joy and enlightenment to a grateful world.

Carl R. Mueller
School of Theater, Film and Television
Department of Theater
University of California, Los Angeles

Introduction

Edward Albee was the unwanted and often renegade adopted son of two wealthy Westchester conservatives. This conflict between the placid world of convention and the uncontrollable forces boiling beneath his surface would someday be seen as the continuing tension of his plays. If we are to believe the playwright, Albee's adoptive parents were like Ibsen's *Pillars of Society* (1875–77) — outwardly respectable, inwardly contemptible. As a high school dropout, a dedicated alcoholic, and a gay man — and as one who sympathized profoundly with the oppressed of the world — Albee seemed to form his very identity in the conflict between the suburban square and the Bohemian hipster.

From the moment Peter confronts Jerry on a Village park bench in *The Zoo Story* (1958), Albee's first American success, this conflict is clear. If Jerry at first seems to be the menace, it is Peter who proves to be the murderer. Jerry impales himself on the knife he places in Peter's hand, thus forcing him to confront the demons beneath his respectable surface.

It would be wrong, however, to assume that Albee is simply satirizing the shopping mall world of convention. He is a product both of suburbia and Bohemia, and his futile efforts to resolve these warring elements within himself often create the drama of his plays. Take one of his masterpieces, *Who's Afraid of Virginia Woolf* (1961–62), for example. George and Martha are presumably named after the father and mother of our country. But instead of representing a united front of patriotism and respectability, this couple is embroiled in the most tumultuous marital strife perhaps in all dramatic literature. Or perhaps that distinction should be reserved for that earlier curdled relationship between Agamemnon and Clytemnestra in *The Oresteia* (458 B.C.), because, unlike Aeschylus, Albee shows us the genuine bond of love beneath the searing sexual hatred.

In this play, as in much of Albee's work, there is an element of devilry, and often a note of mischief. George aims a shotgun at his wife that transforms into a Japanese parasol. Martha rhapsodizes about a child who proves to be wholly imaginary. Unlike Arthur Miller, who believed that the world of Absurdism threatened the reality of the family play, Albee was among the first (along with Ionesco in *The Bald Soprano*, 1949) to demonstrate that absurdity was very likely a crucial element of the domestic scene. This was a continuing theme in *A Delicate Balance* (1966) and *Everything in the Garden* (1966), where Albee seemed to have momentarily abandoned his redskin attack on fortress America to become a paleface comedian of manners. And it reached some kind of climax in his writing of *The Goat, or Who Is Sylvia?* (2002) where the hero, a happily married family man with a gay son, falls passionately in love with a farmyard animal.

But perhaps the finest example of the wedding of suburbia and Bohemia in Albee, the most poignant revelation of how rebellion can be leavened with the yeast of love, is to be found in his later play, *Three Tall Women* (1991). There, Albee, in the character of a gay returning son, forgives his dying mother for all her meanness, her parsimony, her rejections, her unloving nature. And instead of being impaled on the knife of respectability, as was Jerry in *The Zoo Story* (1958), the son emerges from the experience a wiser, kinder, and more understanding human being.

Biographers have written about the schizoid split in Albee's nature, motivated either by his sobriety or drunkeness. This is yet another example of the rift in his nature between the good boy and the demon, the family man and the sexual desperado, the spirit that affirms and the spirit that denies. However much unhappiness these conflicts have caused him in his personal life, they are the stuff out of which great drama has been made.

Robert Brustein
Founding Director of the Yale and American Repertory Theatres
Distinguishing Scholar in Residence, Suffolk University
Senior Research Fellow, Harvard University

Albee

IN A MINUTE

A snapshot of the playwright's world. From historical events to pop-culture and the literary landscape of the time, this brief list catalogues events that directly or indirectly impacted the playwright's writing. Play citations refer to opening or premiere dates.

Albee

HIS WORKS

PLAYS

The Zoo Story
The Death of Bessie Smith
The Sandbox
FAM and YAM
The American Dream
Who's Afraid of Virginia Woolf?
Tiny Alice
A Delicate Balance
Box and *Quotations From Chairman Mao Tse-Tung*
All Over
Seascape
Counting the Ways and *Listening: Two Plays*
The Lady from Dubuque
The Man Who Had Three Arms
Finding the Sun
The Marriage Play
Three Tall Women
The Lorca Play
Fragments: A Sit Around
The Play About the Baby
The Goat, or Who Is Sylvia?
Knock, Knock, Who's There?
Peter and Jerry (Homelife and *The Zoo Story)*
Occupant
Me, Myself, and I

This section presents a complete list of the playwright's works in chronological order by world premiere date.

ADAPTATIONS

The Ballad of the Sad Café

Malcolm

Breakfast at Tiffany's (music/lyrics by Bob Merrill)

Everything in the Garden

Lolita

OPERA, ONE-ACT

Bartleby (music by William Flanagan)

ESSAYS

Albee, Edward. *Stretching My Mind: The Collected Essays 1960–2005*. New York: Carroll and Graf, 2005.

COLLECTIONS

Albee, Edward. *Collected Plays of Edward Albee: 1958–1965*. Vol 1. New York: Overlook, 2004.

Albee, Edward. *Collected Plays of Edward Albee: 1966–1977*. Vol. 2. New York: Overlook, 2004.

Albee, Edward. *Collected Plays of Edward Albee: 1978–2003*. Vol. 3. New York: Overlook, 2006.

Onstage with Albee

Introducing Colleagues and
Contemporaries of Edward Albee

 THEATER

Samuel Beckett, Irish playwright
Jerzy Grotowski, Polish director
Uta Hagen, German/American actor
John Osborne, English playwright
Harold Pinter, English playwright
Alan Schneider, American director
Neil Simon, American playwright
Tom Stoppard, English playwright

 ARTS

Leonard Bernstein, American composer
Chuck Berry, American musician
Maria Callas, American singer
Miles Davis, American musician
Philip Glass, American composer
Roy Lichtenstein, American artist
Elvis Presley, American singer
Andy Warhol, American pop artist

 FILM

Woody Allen, American filmmaker
Marlon Brando, American actor
Judy Garland, American singer

This section gives a list of contemporaries, whom the playwright may or may not have known. This can help you understand the intellectual, cultural, and historical times the playwright lived in. Eight contemporaries are shown in each category.

Stanley Kubrick, American filmmaker
Marilyn Monroe, American actor
Mike Nichols, German/American filmmaker
Roman Polanski, Polish/American filmmaker
Franco Zeffirelli, Italian filmmaker and stage director

POLITICS/MILITARY

Fidel Castro, Cuban president
Mikhail Gorbachev, Russian political leader
Saddam Hussein, Iraqi president
John F. Kennedy, American president
Martin Luther King Jr., American civil rights leader
Henry Kissinger, American statesman
Margaret Thatcher, English prime minister
Malcolm X, American activist

SCIENCE

Seymour Cray, American computer designer
Francis Crick, English molecular biologist
Jane Goodall, English zoologist
R. D. Laing, Scottish psychiatrist
Stanley Milgram, American psychologist
Luc Montagnier, French virologist
Carl Sagan, American astronomer
James Watson, American biochemist

LITERATURE

Maya Angelou, American writer
Truman Capote, American writer
Anne Frank, Dutch diarist
Allen Ginsberg, American poet
Gabriel García Márquez, Colombian writer
Susan Sontag, American writer

Gore Vidal, American writer
Elie Wiesel, Romanian/American writer

RELIGION/PHILOSOPHY
Roland Barthes, French literary theorist
Noam Chomsky, American philosopher/linguist
Jacques Derrida, Algerian/French philosopher
Jerry Falwell, American evangelist
Jügen Habermas, German philosopher
Billy Graham, American evangelist
Pope John Paul II, Polish pope
Bstandzin rgyamtsho, 14th Dalai Lama, Tibetan religious leader

SPORTS
Roger Bannister, English runner
Wilt Chamberlain, American basketball player
Joe DiMaggio, American baseball player
Joe Louis, American boxer
Rocky Marciano, American boxer
Mickey Mantle, American baseball player
Arnold Palmer, American golfer
Jackie Robinson, American baseball player

INDUSTRY/BUSINESS
Helen Gurley Brown, American publisher
Malcolm Forbes, American publisher
Hugh Hefner, American publisher
Robert Maxwell, Czech/American publisher
Rupert Murdoch, Australian global media mogul
David Rockefeller, American banker
Ted Turner, American media tycoon
Warren Buffet, American investor

ALBEE

in an hour

FOUNDLING

Edward Albee is fond of saying that he was bought for $133.30, his adoption fees. Little is known of Albee's birth mother, Louise Harvey, but on March 12, 1928, she gave birth to a son in either Washington, D.C., or northern Virginia. According to the adoption papers, the father of the baby had "deserted and abandoned both the mother and child." His biological mother gave him up for adoption, and he was delivered to the Alice Chapin Adoption Nursery in Manhattan. On March 30, at eighteen days old, he was placed with Reed A. Albee and Frances ("Frankie") C. Albee, who brought him back to their home in Westchester, N.Y. After living with the Albees for ten months, he was formally adopted on February 1, 1929, and named Edward Franklin Albee III, after Reed's father, Edward Franklin Albee II, who had been the cofounder of the Keith-Albee chain of vaudeville theaters. It was not a match made in heaven.

This is the core of the book. The essay places the playwright in the context of his or her world and analyzes the influences and inspirations within that world.

POOR LITTLE RICH KID

The Albees lived in a grand manor house, which bordered the water in exclusive Larchmont on the Long Island Sound, complete with fabulous lawns and large trees. Albee's adoptive parents, Reed and Frankie, were wealthy, Republican WASPs who were into the good life. Edward provided the required heir. Reed Albee was a short man with a glass eye, who loved tall women, was notoriously unfaithful, and was content living off the family fortune. Frankie, Reed's third wife, was beautiful, six-foot in her heels, and vivacious. She also displayed the kind of casual bigotry that was common in those decades.

Little Edward was showered with expensive toys (Grenadier Guard toy soldiers, a four-foot-long model sailboat, electric trains), had a St. Bernard, rode the family horses, took tennis lessons with a tennis champion, had boxing lessons with a paid companion, and swam in the ocean nearby.

His nanny encouraged his interest in the arts; they'd listen to the Metropolitan Opera on the radio and were chauffeured by limousine to New York City to see Broadway shows (seeing his first show at seven, *Jumbo*, with Jimmy Durante). Ed Wynn was a friend of the family when young Edward was taken to see him; in *Hooray for What!* Wynn ad-libbed Edward's name in a long list of people his character was saying hello to on the phone. Albee remembers loving the absurd elements in Olsen and Johnson's *Hellzapoppin'* (for instance, a plant carried through the audience that got larger each time). Eventually, such absurdities would find their way happily into his plays.

Each winter, the entire extended Albee family would travel down to Palm Beach to Reed's mother's Florida house in her two private rail-cars. In 1940, Grandmother Albee died and left Reed "The Hommocks," a grand estate of nine acres in Larchmont and Edward's favorite boyhood home.

But his parents were emotionally distant, absorbed in their own interests, and focused on the proprieties of their lifestyle. Reportedly, Frankie's favorite punishing remark was to remind Edward he was adopted, inferring he could be returned, and exclaiming, "Just you wait until you're eighteen, and I'll have you out of here so fast it will make your head spin." The contrast between the gracious façade of his socially conscious American family and the ugly reality beneath was not lost on young Edward, as his plays would so brilliantly demonstrate. He seems to have had only two relatives for whom he felt a lifelong affection. The first was Grandma Cotter, Frankie's mother, who lived with them. As Albee told Carol Rocamora in a 2008 interview in *Theatre Magazine*: "She was the only one in the family I cared about. She was being pushed to one side, so we were in league against the enemy in the middle [his parents]. She liked me. She smoked a lot, had a Pekinese and a good sense of humor." At twelve, he was the family bartender, making his grandmother old-fashioneds at cocktail time. He also had an Aunt Jane, Frankie's younger sister, who visited often and, although alcoholic, connected with the boy.

There were other children in the neighborhood, many of whom played with Albee because he was the richest kid on the block, but Noel Farrand was a neighbor's son and the nearest thing to a sibling Albee ever had; they wandered the houses, gardens, and woods together and remained lifelong friends. Albee would later dedicate his play *Tiny Alice* to Farrand.

SCHOOL DAYS

Once Albee reached school age, he attended Rye Country Day School, except when visiting Palm Beach, where he attended the Palm Beach Private School. In 1940, at twelve, in keeping with children of the moneyed class, he was sent to The Lawrenceville School, an all-boys preparatory school in New Jersey. But he only showed up for classes that interested him and made poor grades. He did get some practical theater experience while there; he appeared in a Noel Coward one-act (playing a middle-aged dowager). Before the end of his sophomore year, he was dismissed for not attending classes. In exasperation, his parents sent him to the Valley Forge Military Academy in Pennsylvania. Edward remembered it as essentially a reform school, although he did write poetry that was published in the school newspaper. After a year and a half, he left Valley Forge due to both academic and health reasons (measles and chicken pox, among others).

In 1944, he transferred to Choate, an exclusive, all-boys prep school in Wallingford, Connecticut. Albee was admitted but only because the Lawrenceville headmaster wrote to Choate's headmaster on his behalf. Mel Gussow, Albee's biographer, quotes from the letter: "Ed is an adopted child and, very confidentially, he dislikes his mother with a cordial and eloquent dislike which I consider entirely justified. . . . She is, however, in my opinion a selfish, dominating person, whereas Ed is a sensitive, perceptive and intelligent boy. . . . I can think of no other boy who, I believe, has been so fully the victim of an unsympathetic home background or who has exhibited so fully the psychological effect of feeling that he is not wanted." While at Choate, he published in the Choate literary magazine and was its managing editor. He was also the music editor and reviewer for *Choate News*. Albee acted in *Androcles and the Lion*, and he was active on the debating team and had a program playing music on the school's radio station.

After graduating from high school, Albee attempted college, but he did not try very hard. He entered Trinity College in Hartford, Connecticut. Rather than attending his required freshman classes, he audited upper division courses that interested him, such as nineteenth-century literature. He also joined a theater group, the Jesters, appearing in Clifford Odets's *Golden Boy* and Maxwell Anderson's *Masque of Kings*. After three semesters of skipping classes, he was dismissed.

After Trinity, in 1948, he worked at the Warwick and Legler advertising agency in New York City as an office boy. He tried to write advertising copy but was unsuccessful. Around 1949, he took a few classes at Columbia, among them a short-story writing class.

THE WRITER AS A YOUNG MAN

As a child attending Lawrenceville, his future writing career seems to have gotten its start. There he wrote poetry and a three-act farce called *Aliqueen* (which his mother threw away). In 1945, while attending Choate, Albee had his first publication, a poem, in *Kaleidograph*, a Texas monthly. It echoed the poems typical of fraught teenage poets (although with some cadences reminiscent of T. S. Eliot, an early influence): "You must let me live! / I have not as yet begun . . . / The world has need of life, not death. / And I have not yet begun." At Choate he wrote his first novel, *The Flesh of Unbelievers*, and next two plays. The 537-page novel was about a brilliant young man misunderstood by his parents. At his friend Noel Farrand's request (who was attending a strict Catholic prep school), Albee wrote his second play, *Schism*, a one-act about the rebellion of a young Irish couple against Roman Catholic and Irish customs. His third play was an eleven-page one-act play, called *Each in His Own Way*. Set in Nazi-occupied Poland, it was about a Chopin-loving piano teacher saving his prize pupil. These works were clearly the handicraft of a writer-in-training, but they were important because reading and emulating the great writers provided the young man with a course of action. Albee would never stop writing. As quoted by Gussow, when he returned to Choate to receive the Seal Prize in 1972, Albee declared: "I didn't come to Choate to study. . . . I came to Choate to learn how to educate myself: that, I consider, to be the function of an educational institution . . . For better or worse, Choate was the only educational institution I ever went to where I began to get a glimmering of how I could educate myself."

LIKE A DUCK TO WATER

Albee has never been shy about his sexual orientation, although he was never one to advertise or agitate for the cause. If asked, he'd tell the truth. According to Albee, he was eight when he first realized he liked boys; he had a crush on the groom's son. It was at Lawrenceville that

Albee believes he had his first sexual encounter with an older boy. He told his biographer, Mel Gussow, that he "took to it, as they say, as a duck to water." However, like many who were raised in an environment and time when homosexuality was never mentioned but utterly condemned, Albee did try out the opposite sex. In 1945 he met Celeste Seymour; they dated a couple of years: clubs, dancing, and underage drinking. She was seen as a suitable match; fortunately they drifted apart. He says he slept with three different women at Trinity College but was also visiting the gay bars in Hartford. Around 1946–47, he joined the reserves to avoid being drafted but was called to the draft board. Asked if he was a homosexual, he said "yes," and they never contacted him again. However, he also dated a childhood friend's sister, Delphine, and was her escort for her 1949 coming-out party. They discussed marriage and were informally engaged. But he ended it when he realized how deceitful it was. As Albee observed to Gussow, "For God's sake, what did I think I was doing? I was going to bed with boys from age thirteen on and enjoyed it greatly." In 1949, that decision was an act of courage that many gay men of that era never made. In a 2003 interview with Stephen Bottoms, in *The Cambridge Companion to Edward Albee*, Albee said that he did not "see that much difference between heterosexual and homosexual relationships, if they are two people really involved with each other, trying to make a life together. I don't see that much difference, except that the homosexual couple have to fight a lot of prejudices, and illegalities."

LEAVING HOME

After flunking out of college, Albee returned home and the antagonism between him and his parents increased. His mother began to read his letters. Their fights intensified. (She once threw a crystal ashtray at him). In 1949, after a night of drinking, he arrived home at five in the morning with vomit in the car. He went upstairs to bed, leaving the lights on in the driveway. (This scene later appeared in *A Delicate Bal-*

ance.) He was awakened and dressed down by his parents for leaving a mess for the servants to clean up. Accusations increased: for his failure in college, for not liking their friends, for leaving those driveway lights on. While his homosexuality was never discussed and Albee was not "out" in the traditional sense, it nevertheless must have played a part in his parents' anger — parents often suspect, even when the "h" word has not been spoken aloud. The twenty-one-year-old Albee went upstairs, packed a bag, called a taxi to take him to the train station, and left home. The rift was a serious one. He never talked to his father again, and he did not see his mother for seventeen years. When his beloved Grandma Cotter died ten years later in 1959, his parents did not tell him, and Albee missed her funeral.

DOWN AND "OUT" IN THE VILLAGE

Albee moved to Greenwich Village in 1949 and roomed for a short while with his childhood friend Noel Farrand, who was now a struggling composer. Conveniently, the same year he moved to the Village, he turned twenty-one and received a small inheritance from his paternal grandmother, twenty-five dollars a week. This, combined with a series of jobs designed not to get in the way of his nightlife, supported his Bohemian lifestyle. He worked as a clerk in a record store, allowing students and himself to steal books and musical scores, and he adjusted the cash register to pay himself a few extra dollars a day. He also worked in the record department at Bloomingdale's and the book department at Gimbels Department Store. He moved from apartment to apartment, from Greenwich Village to Chelsea, just north of the Village. In 1955, he began delivering telegrams for Western Union. He liked the work because there was lots of walking, a flexible work schedule, and pretty good money when tips were factored into his salary.

In 1948, when Albee was twenty, he met the twenty-five-year-old composer and music critic William Flanagan. Four years later they rented an apartment together after becoming lovers on a trip to

Italy. Their relationship was tumultuous and intense. Together they led the lush life, in every sense of the word. Flanagan was a star in the heavy-drinking, sexually active subculture of the gay world in 1950s New York City. They hung out in gay bars and bathhouses, partying and drinking to excess with friends. Albee would later attribute his struggles with alcoholism to these years. Flanagan was Albee's first serious love relationship and his most trusted critic and teacher.

New York City also served as his mentor and teacher. In a 2004 article in *The Guardian* by Aida Edemariam, Albee described what the Village was like during those days: "I found myself surrounded by people who were creative, painters and sculptors and composers and writers. A lot of experimental theater was going on, so you could educate yourself. That was a feast. Everybody was poor, and nobody was famous. All things seemed young, and open and really good." Artists like William de Kooning and Jackson Pollock, and writers like James Agee and Allen Ginsberg could be seen drinking and talking at their favorite bar, and restaurants such as the Cedar Tavern and San Remo. Furthermore, his job delivering telegrams for Western Union provided him with a portrait gallery of human types and experiences.

During these years, Albee continued to write, although he saw himself as principally a poet. In fact, at Farrand's urging, he showed up on W. H. Auden's doorstep and had the youthful audacity to hand Auden a stack of poetry, asking him to read it. Auden did. Later, he showed his poems to Thornton Wilder, who suggested that this aspiring poet should write plays instead. Albee responded by writing a verse play, *The Making of a Saint*, which takes place in a way station between heaven and hell. He dedicated it to Wilder, but nothing came of it. During these important and formative years, from 1949 to 1958, Albee wrote nine plays, dozens of stories, and over one hundred poems. By his own admission, none of them were very good. Then, everything changed.

THE ZOO OF *THE ZOO*

As his thirtieth birthday approached in 1958, Albee knew that he would be receiving the principal of $100,000 from his paternal grandmother's trust. This meant that he was liberated from the need to work and had the freedom to devote himself entirely to his lifestyle and to writing.

Albee has often described as his thirtieth birthday present to himself not the typewriter he stole from Western Union, but what he did with it. He used it to begin to write in his own voice. One month before his birthday, he sat down in a folding chair in the kitchen of his apartment and wrote the play that would change his life. It began, "I've been to the zoo. I said I've been to the zoo. MISTER, I'VE BEEN TO THE ZOO!" Albee wrote *The Zoo Story* in two-and-a-half weeks, made pencil revisions, retyped it, and finished it two days before his birthday. The play became a watershed moment in American theater history, inspiring a whole generation of playwrights, among them Tom Stoppard, Sam Shepard, David Mamet, Terrence McNally, Lanford Wilson, and John Guare. As quoted by Gussow, Guare observed: "We all wrote our own version of *Zoo Story*. Albee spawned an entire generation of park-bench plays. Theater for years became littered with park benches. To show you were avant-garde, you needed no more than a dark room and a park bench."

Zoo Story's action focuses on two characters: Peter, a buttoned-up executive who has steadfastly chosen to live a life-not-examined, and Jerry, an agitated recluse, who insists that life, with all its joys and miseries, must be fully experienced. Jerry, desperate to have a real conversation with another human being, forces Peter to listen to stories about Jerry's life, including the famous "Story of Jerry and the Dog." Their fateful meeting in New York City's Central Park reaches its climax after Peter announces that he's going home, thus threatening to cut off the possibility of further contact. After tickling Peter and then forcing him off the bench, Jerry drops a knife in front of the now angry Peter, who grabs the knife in self-defense. In a final, desperate act, Jerry impales himself on the knife in Peter's hand, killing himself and sending the horrified Peter back to his middle-class life: one must assume a changed man.

The Zoo Story has been variously interpreted. Peter has been seen as representative of a disengaged America, isolating itself from the rest of the world. Peter and Jerry have been identified as representative of the relationship between Albee's distant father and himself. Albee once observed that Peter was his former, Larchmont self, while Peter was his New York City self. The characters have been described as a comparison of the Eisenhower era and Kennedy era. In perhaps one of the best-known interpretations, Jerry has been seen as a Christ figure, sacrificing himself for the good of humanity (Peter).

Quite atypical of a new American play in 1959, it received its world premiere at Berlin's Schiller Theater in a double bill with Samuel Beckett's *Krapp's Last Tape*, and it was performed in German. Albee was present for the performance, understanding not a word of the German translation. There was total silence after the heartstopping moment when Jerry forces Peter to stab him, and then there was wild applause. It was a hit in Germany, but what of America? As Albee wrote in "On *The Zoo Story*," a 1960 essay in *Stretching My Mind*: "Careers are funny things. They begin mysteriously and, just as mysteriously, they can end; and I am at just the very beginning of what I hope will be a long and satisfying life in the theater."

MOVING ON FROM FIRST LOVE

Just before sailing to Germany in September of 1959 to see the premiere of *Zoo Story*, Albee and Flanagan split after seven years. In February 1959, Albee had met the nineteen-year-old Terrence McNally at a party. Albee soon moved into McNally's apartment. But Albee and Flanagan remained friends and collaborated. He would remain one of Albee's most insightful critics until his death.

"BOY" WONDER

By 1960, Broadway had become so expensive that risky works no longer opened there, therefore the Off-Broadway movement emerged, and it was ripe for the type of experimental theater that was already well under way on the continent. In addition, John F. Kennedy had just been elected president, and the "Camelot" years infused the nation with youthful enthusiasm.

Appropriately, the same theater that provided Eugene O'Neill with his first American premiere also provided Albee with his — the Provincetown Playhouse. *The Zoo Story* opened on January 14, 1960, again pairing with *Krapp's Last Tape*, this time in English.

As would prove to be the case with the vast of majority of Albee's plays, *The Zoo Story* received widely mixed reviews. However, Albee was hailed as part of a new and exciting wave of theater. His first produced play won the Obie Award and the Vernon Rice Award. Pictures of the brooding young man were sent by his producer, Richard Barr, to newspapers and magazines to promote the play, and everyone that was anyone recognized him.

In rapid succession, the suddenly hot playwright had a series of openings in 1960. *The Death of Bessie Smith* was based on the tragic death of blues singer Bessie Smith and set in the white hospital where she was refused admission. It premiered, like *The Zoo Story*, not in America, but overseas, in Berlin, which was not entirely inappropriate since the playwright has acknowledged that it has a somewhat Brechtian structure.

The Sandbox premiered in May at the Jazz Gallery in New York City, with a score by William Flanagan. Only fourteen minutes long in production (and reportedly Albee's personal favorite), it was written while Albee was working on *The American Dream*. In fact, four characters (Mommy, Daddy, Grandma, and the Young Man) were lifted from the yet-to-be-produced *The American Dream* and placed on a beach, with the Young Man being reinvented as the Angel of Death. The character of Grandma was inspired by his Grandmother

Cotter, and the play is dedicated to her. In the play, as in life, the grandma lives with her daughter and son-in-law, "They moved me into the big town house with *them*. . . ."

Premiering in August at The White Barn in Connecticut, *FAM and YAM*, which stands for "Famous American Playwright" and "Young American Playwright, was Albee's fourth play to premiere in 1960. It was apparently inspired by Albee's visit to famous American playwright William Inge. The older playwright was appalled when he read the published script in *Harper's Bazaar.*

AMERICAN DREAM

With each play (even *FAM and YAM*, which was considered a trifle precious), Albee's reputation grew. With the production of *The American Dream* in 1961, Albee further established himself as a young American playwright to be taken seriously. However, *Bartleby* (a curtain-raiser for *American Dream* and Albee's first adaptation) was not well received. It was a one-act operatic version of Melville's short story, with music by Flanagan. Producer Richard Barr quickly replaced it with a dance piece and then with the American premiere of *The Death of Bessie Smith*. As 1961 was at the height of America's Civil Rights Movement, this play resonated more with the times.

The American Dream, like *The Sandbox*, takes elements of the playwright's own family and reinvents them through the lens of the Absurd Theater in order to comment on the family of America. There is witty Grandma, shuttled to the side and studiously ignored: "doddering there in the corner." There is bossy Mommy and the emasculated Daddy. They adopted a child long ago (their "bumble of joy"). He turned out to be more trouble than he was worth, so they mutilated and killed him. Mrs. Barker, perhaps of the Bye-Bye Adoption Agency, drops by for a visit. Some audience members were shocked by the invitation Mommy extends to her guest, Mrs. Barker, "Are you sure you're comfortable? Won't you take off your dress?" — and Mrs. Barker's response, "I don't mind if I do," and the subsequent removal of her dress. Finally a gorgeous young man (who will do anything for money) appears: He is the "American Dream." He turns out to be the far more acceptable adult twin of the long ago, murdered child. Mommy notes, however, that he still has a way to go to be acceptable: "You must learn to count. We're a wealthy family, and you must learn to count." Grandma escapes, the American Dream stays on, and, as Grandma says, ". . . everybody's got what he thinks he wants."

The American Dream went on to become one of Albee's signature plays (receiving a red, white, and blue revival directed by Albee himself in 2008). Martin Esslin, in his definitive 1961 work, *The Theatre of the Absurd*, famously labeled *The American Dream* as the first American play (and Albee the first American playwright) of the Absurd Theater. Esslin maintains that the play "squarely attacks the ideals of progress, optimism, and faith in the national mission, and pours scorn on the sentimental ideals of family life, togetherness, and physical fitness; the euphemistic language and unwillingness to face the ultimate facts of the human condition that in America . . . represent the essence of bourgeois assumptions and attitudes." Albee has confirmed that the first few minutes of *American Dream* is an homage to absurdist playwright Eugène Ionesco's *The Bald Soprano*. Mommy and Daddy echo the opening dialogue of Mr. and Mrs. Smith in Ionesco's breakthrough play. Albee has also gleefully acknowledged that Burr Tillstrom's puppet show, *Kukla, Fran and Ollie*, served as an inspiration. He sees casting Kukla as Daddy, Madame Oglepuss as Mommy, Fran Allison as Mrs. Barker, Oliver J. Dragon as the American Dream, and Beula (Albee's favorite) as Grandma.

In his 1961 introduction to the first edition of *The American Dream*, Albee takes umbrage at certain critics who found *Dream* too distasteful. He goes on to defend his fifth play: "And just what is the *content* of *The American Dream* (a comedy, yet) that so upsets these guardians of public morality? The play is an examination of the American Scene, an attack on the substitution of artificial for real values in our society, a condemnation of complacence, cruelty, emasculation and vacuity; it is a stand against the fiction that everything in this slipping land of ours is peachy-keen. Is the play offensive? I certainly hope so; it was my intention to offend — as well as amuse and entertain. Is it nihilist, immoral, defeatist? Well, to that let me answer that *The American Dream* is a picture of our time — as I see it, of course."

The American Dream marked the first time (of many) that Alan Schneider directed an Albee premiere. In *Stretching My Mind*, a 1992 essay, written eight years after Schneider's death, Albee credits his long-time collaborator for teaching him, not how to write, but how to *be* a playwright: "When Alan and I began working on *The American Dream* . . . I had not learned that I was expected to know what I had done. I had assumed that having done it was sufficient . . . . I was expected to be able to answer every single question that he asked me about not only the intention of the play, the intention of the particular situation in the play, but the characters themselves, their nature, their background. Alan would ask me questions that at first surprised me but then ultimately merely revealed that he was trying to get out of me that which I *had*, but had never before articulated. He made me aware that I *did know* the subtext and the history of all the characters that I had written, but I hadn't thought about it."

Schneider, along with William Flanagan and Richard Barr, provided Albee with dedication and support. Sadly, his father, Reed Albee, never demonstrated the supportive love of a father. This distant man died in August of 1961 while Albee was in Rio de Janeiro. He did not return to attend his father's funeral.

THE PLAYWRIGHT OF HIS GENERATION

For his next theatrical feat, Albee finished revising his script originally called "The Exorcism." It was written during a period when anything seemed possible for both America and the suddenly renowned playwright. But nothing could have prepared him for what happened when his first full-length play (extra-full-length, at over three hours running time) premiered. Albee, with the support of his faithful producers, Barr and Clinton Wilder, determined that *Who's Afraid of Virginia Woolf?* would open on Broadway. It was the first successful move of a playwright from Off Broadway to Broadway. It opened at the Billy Rose Theater on October 13, 1962, under the direction of Schneider and starring the formidable Uta Hagen as Martha. Opening night was rainy, but all the New York critics were there, as were John Steinbeck and Tennessee Williams (the latter would return to see it several more times). The production shocked Broadway audiences, who nevertheless made it a runaway financial success. The first two weeks of the run must have been quite alarming in other ways as well; the Cuban Missile Crisis erupted two days after the opening and was not resolved until October 28 by President Kennedy.

The title of the play came from remembered soap graffiti on a bar mirror in the Village. "Virginia Woolf," of course, references the English writer. (In fact, Albee wrote her widower, asking for permission to use her name. Leonard Woolf came to see the London production.) The three acts are each given their own title: "Fun and Games," "Walpurgisnacht" (which references witches and pagan rites of spring), and "The Exorcism." Savagely cruel, but often funny, game playing is at the heart of this work, and each game was given an appropriate name. And just as games are an amusing substitution for real war, the games in *Woolf* have much to do with the characters' need to substitute fiction for reality. As the playwright explained in an interview with C. W. E. Bigsby in 1980, ". . . in the play all that is suggested is that you clear away all the debris and then you decide what you are going to do. It doesn't say that everything is going to be all right at all. O'Neill suggested that you have false illusions in order to survive. The only optimistic act in *Who's Afraid of Virginia Woolf?* is to say, admit that they are false illusions and then live with them if you want and know that they are false. After all, it's an act of public exorcism."

The action is set in a faculty house on a New England college campus of an older married couple, George and Martha (whose names, of course, are those of the founding "parents" of America). A young married couple visit in the wee hours, Nick (who's never called "Nick") and Honey (which may just be what her husband calls her). They battle it out in the living room of the older, unsuccessful history professor and his heavy-drinking wife, the daughter of the college president. As the two couples continue to drink toward dawn, Martha mercilessly attacks George for his various inadequacies ("Humiliate the Host"), and he responds in kind. In Act Two, Martha's attacks continue, and George suggests that it's time to change the game to "Hump the Hostess," but soon George targets Nick and Honey, and he begins to tear down the façades that cover up the truth about their miserable marriage ("Get the Guests"). "Hump the Hostess" finally makes the playing roster, and Martha comes on to Nick in front of George. As Act Two ends, George decides to use the ultimate weapon against Martha, to destroy their most precious fantasy. Act Three promises exorcism and delivers it. Martha admits that she really loves George, "who keeps learning the games we play as quickly as I can change the rules; who can make me happy and I do not wish to be happy, and yes I do wish to be happy. George and Martha: sad, sad, sad." Their final game is "Bringing Up Baby," and George begins to discuss their son. Eventually he announces that Western Union has delivered a telegram, announcing a death. (It should be remembered that Albee delivered such telegrams.) Nick and Honey leave, and George and Martha, tenderly, move into the new day.

As in *The American Dream*, there is the issue of missing children. One of the saving games of Martha and George is the existence of a son, who turns out to never have existed, and whose nonexistence is extinguished at the end of the play when George announces in front of the guests that their son has died. In turn, Nick and Honey's marriage was the result of a false pregnancy; as Nick says, "she blew up, and then she went down."

Albee's biographer and others have noted several aspects of his own life that found their way into *Woolf*, but mining one's own experiences is typical practice for most playwrights, and in no way undermines the shocking originality of this alarmingly naturalistic script. Albee also references other scripts: For instance, George presents flowers for Martha with the words, "Flores para los muertos," a reference to Tennessee Williams' *Streetcar Named Desire*, and Martha mentions "The Poker Night," which was the original title for Williams's play. Also, Martha and George hold an insult contest using French, thus echoing Gogo's and Didi's insult contest in *Waiting for Godot*. Albee has also noted that James Thurber's influence is evident when George mimics Nick and pretends to misunderstand him and when George and Martha are in attack and counterattack mode.

As with most of his plays, *Who's Afraid of Virginia Woolf?* received extremely mixed reviews, provoking either outrage or adoration. Robert Coleman of the *New York Daily Mirror* called it "a sick play for sick people" and a "sordid and cynical dip into depravity." More than one critic compared it to O'Neill's *Long Day's Journey Into Night*, and in subsequent years many writers have been unable to withstand the temptation to refer to *Woolf* as Albee's "long night's journey into day." But with its publication, not only theater critics but also scholars began to pay attention to the thirty-four-year-old playwright. Thanks to the 1966 film starring Elizabeth Taylor and Richard Burton, *Who's Afraid of Virginia Woolf?* is Albee's most widely known script, and it has also received several successful revivals.

He was now declared the playwright of his generation and joined the ranks of Eugene O'Neill, Tennessee Williams, and Arthur Miller. The February 1963 *Newsweek* cover story featured a picture of Albee as an "angry young man" with the cover banner of "Playwright Edward Albee: Odd Man In." After *Who's Afraid of Virginia Woolf?*, it was Albee, Tennessee Williams, and Arthur Miller opening new plays on Broadway for several years. Ironically, despite *Woolf*'s full houses, five Antoinette Perry "Tony" Awards, the New York Drama Critics' Award, and many other awards, the trustees of the Pulitzer Prize Committee overrode the judgment of their own drama jury and denied Albee the prize. They would try and make up for it later.

The production made money for everyone associated with it, and it continued to provide Albee with the freedom to pursue only what he chose to for years to come. Albee bought a seaside house in Montauk Point, Long Island. With additional proceeds, he and producers Barr and Wilder also started the Playwrights Unit, which operated for eight years and helped develop the talents of playwrights by providing a theater (the Cherry Lane), actors, directors, and a production of their plays in front of an invited audience. Scripts by Mart Crowley, Terrence McNally, Lanford Wilson, Sam Shepard, John Guare, Paul Zindel, and others were produced.

Now, as a famous American playwright, Albee joined PEN, an association of writers whose stated goal is to advance literature and defend free expression. Albee would go on to become a major spokesman for oppressed dissident writers, even visiting them in their home countries and seeking ways to bring them to America.

WOOLF AT THE DOOR

The theater world eagerly looked forward to another *Who's Afraid of Virginia Woolf?*; they were disappointed. Albee had other plans. As he wrote in the program notes of the 1996 London revival, *Woolf* has "hung about my neck like a shining medal of some sort — really nice but a trifle onerous."

The playwright followed the astounding success of his first full-length play with an adaptation of Carson McCullers's *Ballad of the Sad Café*: a Southern Gothic novella that centers on Miss Amelia and the dwarf who teaches her to love, the ex-con husband who teaches her the opposite, and her café. In the novella, an anonymous third-person narrator tells the story. To circumvent this problem, Albee's adaptation makes use of a narrator, originally meant to be a recording of McCullers herself, but her deteriorating health prevented this. It was decided that the narrator would be performed by an actor, Roscoe Lee Browne. The formidable Colleen Dewhurst played the equally formidable Miss Amelia.

Albee and McCullers shared an emotional connection, which is apparent in this underappreciated work. Of McCullers, Albee wrote in "Carson McCullers," a 1963 essay in *Scratching My Mind*: "Examine this: she is a lady, who, at an age when most girls have nothing more on their minds than their next cotillions, can conjure a work like *The Ballad of the Sad Café* — a work of great wisdom . . . who, as a girl, trained as a concert pianist until she discovered that the keyboard of the typewriter, when played with magic, produced a music wilder and more beautiful than any other instrument."

Schneider directed. The rehearsal period was difficult as the members of the cast were unsatisfied with the script. Colleen Dewhurst neither liked nor respected Schneider. She secretly consulted with her husband, George C. Scott, who, among other things, helped restage a fight scene and edit down the narrator's ever-growing speeches. Roscoe Lee Browne agreed and, concealing Scott's contributions, requested of both Schneider and Albee to be allowed to cut his speeches. Albee graciously agreed to almost all of the cuts.

While *Who's Afraid of Virginia Woolf?* was still enjoying tremendous success on Broadway, *The Ballad of the Sad Café* premiered on October 30, 1963. McCullers attended the opening in a wheelchair (she died less than four years later). Yet again, reviews were mixed, with adjectives ranging from "tedious" to "magnificent." But *Ballad* did not have the notoriety of *Woolf's* narrative, and the production closed after 123 performances. Albee was deeply disappointed. As quoted by Gussow, he wrote in a letter to Flanagan that he was as fond of this play "as anyone would be of a lovely child who has leukemia . . . ."

AMERICA'S REPRESENTATIVE

Albee met President John F. Kennedy about a month after *Who's Afraid of Virginia Woolf?* opened, and, as noted, John Steinbeck had attended its opening night. (In fact, he wrote Albee a very complimentary letter about the production.) On November 3, 1964, in the middle of the Cold War, Albee left for Moscow to join John Steinbeck as part of President Kennedy's cultural exchange program. Steinbeck had recommended Albee partially because he and Albee had differing political views. The two became close friends.

The writers gave talks and were interviewed, met with both approved and dissident writers, drank vodka, and visited locations in Russia, both those on the itinerary and others of particular interest. It was this trip that seems to have started Albee on a lifelong road of activism for oppressed writers. Upon his return, Albee approached PEN about continuing the cultural exchange by inviting Soviet writers to the United States. As a result, a Soviet delegation visited in November 1964.

Albee was on a side trip to Odessa (to see the famous steps from the seminal film *The Battleship Potemkin*) when he learned of the assassination of President Kennedy. Gussow observes that in a letter to Flanagan, Albee noted how unreal Kennedy's death must have seemed in New York City, but how more so it was to comprehend such devastating news in Russia. It was not so unreal, however, that Albee was unmoved; he observed that he cried "like a child (or maybe like a grownup)."

Personal devastation also awaited Albee on his return to America; he and Terrence McNally separated after a five-year relationship. McNally had become involved with another man. It was an excruciating separation, and it would be years before they were able to come together again, but eventually they renewed their relationship as good friends.

GO ASK ALICE

Dedicated to his childhood friend, Noel Farrand, *Tiny Alice* premiered on Broadway in 1964 under Schneider's direction to critical confusion.

In fact, Albee's play not only perplexed the critics, but the audience, cast, and scholars as well. As a result, a massive amount has been written by critics and scholars alike in an attempt to explain it.

The location is a mansion, and on the set is a model of the mansion that itself, supposedly, contains ever-smaller models of itself. It is suggested that the model is more real than the mansion the characters inhabit (what goes on in the house also seems to occur in the model: a fire, lights going on and off). A rich woman, Miss Alice (who first pretends to be an old woman until she reveals herself to be young and beautiful), will donate a vast amount to the church if Julian, a chaste but sexually alluring young lay brother, will abandon his plans for the priesthood and marry her. When the marriage is concluded, Miss Alice explains that she is not real and that he married the real Alice, who, he is told, is inside the dollhouse mansion. He protests, is shot, and abandoned. During a long, confessional monologue (which the actor desperately wanted shortened), the sound of an ever-louder heartbeat and breathing is heard, and the script's directions note that a "great shadow, or darkening, fills the stage," and that Julian "notices his engulfment." Julian sees something in the darkness and addresses it: "The bridegroom waits for thee, my Alice . . . is thine. O Lord, my God, I have awaited thee, have served thee in thy . . . Alice? ALICE? . . . GOD? I accept thee, Alice, for thou art come to me. God, Alice . . . I accept thy will." He dies, crucified on the dollhouse mansion.

The original cast starred Irene Worth as Alice, and the wildly miscast sixty-year-old John Gielgud as Julian. As rehearsals got underway, Gielgud realized that while he was intrigued by his character, he did not understand the script or his role. He wanted to withdraw from the cast repeatedly but was sustained, mainly by post-rehearsal brandy and Irene Worth's cheerful encouragement. (Some thirty-three years later, Albee realized that Gielgud was right about the monologue. After seeing a revival in 1997, he shortened Julian's death speech by a third.) Irene Worth also found the script challenging, but she was nevertheless enthusiastic about a play she thought argued against using religion as a way to avoid the mystery of the infinite, unexplainable universe.

In Martin Esslin's *Theatre of the Absurd*, he observed of *Tiny Alice*: "Albee broke new ground in a play which clearly tried to evolve a complex image of man's search for truth and certainty in a constantly shifting world, without ever wanting to construct a complete allegory or to offer any solutions to the questions he raised. . . . What it communicates is a mood, a sense of the mystery, the impenetrable complexity of the universe. And that is precisely what a dramatic poet is after."

MOTHER

In the spring of 1965, Albee and his adoptive mother, "Frankie," after a seventeen-year separation, resumed their tentative relationship. She had had a heart attack and was living lonely and alone. Albee visited her one Sunday, bringing her a brooch as a gift. In the years following, she attended his opening nights, and they visited each other. They never discussed his sexual orientation.

Twenty-six years later (two years after his mother's death), he wrote *Three Tall Women*, a play he concedes was based on his mother. In it, the character A observes: "We have a heart attack; they tell him; he comes back. Twenty plus years? That's a long enough sulk — on both sides. He didn't come back when his father died."

TWO BUSTS AND A PULITZER

In 1966 Albee opened three shows: two that failed miserably, and one that would win him his first Pulitzer Prize. His adaptation of James Purdy's novel *Malcolm* closed after seven performances. (One can understand his affinity with the novel; the main character is an orphan adopted by a rich man, who experiences a quick rise to success.) A musical adaptation of Truman Capote's novel *Breakfast at Tiffany's* closed in previews. (Albee had been brought in to salvage the production with a rewrite but was given only two weeks to do it.) However, the Pulitzer-winning *A Delicate Balance* proved to be one of his best plays.

Dedicated to John Steinbeck, *A Delicate Balance* appears to have roots in Albee's childhood. Gussow notes in his biography that the house resembles "The Hommocks," and the character of Claire channels Albee's mother's sister, Jane (a frequent visitor and an alcoholic). Agnes has elements of Albee's mother, and Tobias echoes Albee's father (he is even described as jingling coins in his pocket, a habit he shared with Reed Albee). In fact, Jessica Tandy and Hume Cronyn, who played the original Agnes and Tobias, were taken by Albee to meet Frankie, his mother, as a means of getting into the world of the play. Gussow also postulates that Albee himself has some characteristics of the daughter, Julia (the unloved child who left home but still feels curiously connected and returns to stay). As Agnes informs Tobias, "You have hope, only, of growing older than you are in the company of your steady wife, your alcoholic sister-in-law and occasional visits . . . from our melancholy Julia."

A Delicate Balance takes place in the living room of an upper-class house where a lot of drinking takes place. A WASP couple, Agnes and Tobias, live with Claire, Agnes's alcoholic sister. Harry and Edna appear at the door, seeking asylum. During a quiet evening at home, an anonymous terror had come over them. Their "best friends in the world," Agnes and Tobias, *must* take them in. But it is clear that the situation is too atypical, too close for comfort. In the second act, the daughter, Julia, returns home, for the fourth time. She also has trouble connecting; she is escaping from failed marriage number four. Discovering that Harry and Edna are in her old room, she throws several fits of pique. Harry eventually admits that were the tables turned, they would not let Agnes and Tobias stay in their house. Tobias, demonstrating the conflicts he feels, delivers an "aria," ending with the following: "YOU BRING YOUR TERROR AND YOU COME IN HERE AND YOU LIVE WITH US! YOU BRING YOUR

PLAGUE! YOU STAY WITH US! I DON'T WANT YOU HERE! I DON'T LOVE YOU! BUT BY GOD. . . YOU STAY!! *(Pause.)* STAY! *(Softer.)* Stay! *(Soft, tears.)* Stay. Please? Stay? *(Pause.)* Stay? Please? Stay?" Harry and Edna leave. The play ends with Agnes gently announcing, "Come now; we can begin our day."

The script, as usual, was both praised and condemned. There was considerable discussion of Albee's often-elevated prose; some found it elegant while others found it arcane. More than one critic thought that the dialogue had dominated the plot and characters, but others noted that this served to highlight the seeming impossibility of connecting with others, even "best friends." Harold Clurman of *The New York Times* (November 13, 1966) proclaimed Albee a "master of stage speech." Several noted similarities to T. S. Eliot's verse plays.

Also of note, Albee's use of parenthetical direction is quite extensive. In *A Delicate Balance*, the majority of the lines have directorial input from the playwright. These range from short and to the point "*(Wrinkles her nose.)*" to extensive "*(The next is an aria. It must have in its performance all the horror and exuberance of a man who has kept his emotions under control too long. Tobias will be carried to the edge of hysteria, and he will find himself laughing, sometimes, while he cries from sheer release. All in all, it is genuine and bravura at the same time, one prolonging the other. I shall try to notate it somewhat.)*" — which he does.

In his introduction to the 1966 edition of *A Delicate Balance*, Albee commented on its ongoing, relevant meaning: "The play concerns — as it always has, in spite of early-on critical misunderstanding — the rigidity and ultimate paralysis which afflicts those who settle in too easily, waking up one day to discover that all the choices they have avoided no longer give them any freedom of choice, and that what choices they do have left are beside the point."

Of winning the 1967 Pulitzer Prize for drama, after having been shut out for *Who's Afraid of Virginia Woolf?*, Albee was understandably conflicted. But he accepted the prize, stating that he wouldn't feel right criticizing it if he didn't accept it.

NEVER REPEATING HIMSELF

Although Albee had just won his first Pulitzer Prize and could still command premieres in Broadway houses, there was a growing unease that he, like Tennessee Williams before him, had already written his best plays.

In 1967, the same year he received his first honorary doctorate, he premiered his fourth adaptation on Broadway, an Americanized version of British playwright Giles Cooper's *Everything in the Garden*. Albee's voice, as is appropriate in an adaptation, was not ascendant. It was not a success, but, ironically, it was optioned for a movie and made Albee a bundle. Along with *Ballad of the Sad Café*, *Everything in the Garden* is the other adaptation that, despite its lack of success during its first run, is considered by many to be a worthy adaptation.

Albee is not one to cater to anyone else's tastes; he follows his own artistic vision. Feeling no need to write for commercial success, his next endeavor would prove to frustrate many critics and audience members, while delighting some scholars. Albee tried his hand at the highly experimental with *Quotations from Chairman Mao Tse-Tung*, which is intended to be preceded and followed by performances of *Box*. They are reminiscent of Beckett's so-called anti-plays.

Box appears to be postapocalyptic; humanity has blown it. In place of actors, there is a large cubed frame on stage (the title character, so to speak) and a disembodied female voice recalls a time when "life was simple." The voice laments on the loss of everything worth saving: "If only they had *told* us! Clearly! When it was clear that we were not only corrupt — for there is nothing that is not, or little — but corrupt to the selfishness, to the corruption that we should die to keep it. . . ." She warns that listening to a suite of musical variations brings tears, "Not from the beauty of it, but from solely that you cry from loss . . . so precious. When art begins to hurt . . . when art begins to hurt, it's time to look around. Yes it is."

In *Quotations from Chairman Mao Tse-Tung*, four actors portray four characters, but they do not interact in the typical sense, nor is there a plot. The setting is the deck of an ocean liner in the middle of the ocean. A minister says nothing (i.e., religion really has nothing to offer) as a Long-Winded Lady recounts to him stories from her life. They are unaware of the other characters. A shabby Old Lady recites a sentimental poem, "Over the Hill to the Poor-House," by nineteenth-century American poet Will Carleton. While she is aware of the other characters, she only speaks to the audience. Chairman Mao quotes from his red book of sayings. Why these four? Richard Amacker suggests in his analysis *Edward Albee* that "they represent the four great modern orders — the rich, the poor, established religion, and communism."

Albee first wrote their monologues out separately and then intercut them. In the 1968 publication of the two plays, he stated he was going for a "musical structure — form and counterpoint." As such, their statements appear to comment on each other. For instance, the Long-Winded Lady recalls "the time the taxi went berserk and killed those people!" and Mao proclaims, "Riding roughshod everywhere, U.S. imperialism has made itself the enemy of the people of the world and has increasingly isolated itself." But ultimately, it is the audience/reader who must impose order and meaning on this intentional chaos.

As always, Albee is quite exact as to how he wants his lines delivered. In his general comments to the 1968 publication, he wrote: "I have indicated, quite precisely . . . by means of commas, periods, semicolons, dashes and dots . . . the speech rhythms. Please observe them carefully, for they were not thrown in, like herbs on a salad, to be mixed about."

Mao and *Box* opened on Broadway at the Billy Rose Theater in September 1968. Broadway had seldom seen the like.

Reviews were not enthusiastic to put it mildly, but Harold Clurman in *The Nation* (March 25, 1968) observed: "we are confronted with banality on three levels: the despair of the middle class, the heartbreak of the dispossessed, the rote of the professionally insurgent. . . . There is a melancholy beauty in this play and genuine feeling without tears. The play convinces me that we have in Albee a dramatist who is still growing. *Box-Mao-Box* is like no other play he has written and like very few others written by anyone else."

EXITS AND ENTRANCES

Albee began to experience personal losses. John Steinbeck died in December 1968. A few months later, William Flanagan, Albee's first partner and one of his most insightful critics, was found dead in his apartment. He had died alone, sometime in the last days of August, apparently from a heart attack and an intemperate lifestyle. Albee resolved to start the William Flanagan Memorial Creative Persons Center, an artists' colony in Montauk. To be in residence, artists have to show "poverty and talent" — the two things that bedeviled Flanagan. Albee purchased property the same year of Flanagan's death and started the memorial center two years later. It is still in operation.

In 1971, Jonathan Thomas entered his life. Albee would later credit Thomas with saving his life. He met the twenty-four-year-old Canadian painter in Toronto. Soon after, Thomas visited New York City and shortly thereafter moved in with Albee. Theirs was to be a long and loving relationship. It was Thomas who eventually helped Albee conquer his alcoholism, which was affecting his writing and his personality. In fact, for many years, Albee had the reputation of being cruel and difficult, verbally and emotionally injuring people. He apologized for such an attack in a letter to his biographer, Gussow, after getting toasted at a dinner party and attacking the producer Joe Papp (and everyone else who got in his way): "By nature, I am a gentle, responsible, useful person, with a few special gifts. With liquor, I am insane. . . . If some of us — all of us? — have, as Agnes speculates in *A Delicate Balance*, a 'dark side to our reason,' then I have it, in spades. It mortifies me — tears me apart — and more than ever because I know it is not . . . *me*." With Jonathan Thomas's help, the real Edward Albee would eventually gain the ascendancy.

LIFE AND DEATH

Following the passing of Steinbeck and Flanagan, Albee clearly had death on his mind. In *All Over*, a famous man lies dying, remaining unseen during the last two hours of his life. Those keeping the deathwatch (the wife, son, daughter, best friend, and mistress) grapple with the loss of meaning, of self, that will be extinguished with his life. C. W. E. Bigsby, in *A Critical Introduction to Twentieth-Century American Drama*, observes that this play "presses even closer to the fact which is the root cause of the absurdity and fear that underlies his characters' actions — death."

It premiered in the massive Martin Beck Theater in 1971, a space the director, John Gielgud, thought unsuited for the play. Critical response was deadly, and audiences stayed away. However, Harold Clurman in *The Nation* (April 12, 1971), as he often did, proved to be one of Albee's champions, calling it "the best American play of several seasons." He noted that *All Over* "conveys an existential shudder which has its origins in the soul's dark solitude."

Albee has said that there are only two things to write about: life and death. *All Over* began as a one-act called "Death" before it was expanded into a full-length play. The companion piece, "Life," was developed into a very long script that was renamed *Seascape*.

Albee began an exploration of evolution and the collective unconscious in 1967, reading books on anthropology and sociology. His house in Montauk faces the ocean, and he often vacationed in the Virgin Islands. Combined, these seem to have inspired him to explore our ancestral ties to the ocean rather than the trees. *Seascape*, which premiered in 1974, was the result.

The setting is a beach. An older married couple, Charlie and Nancy, discuss how their lives will change with retirement and about the devolution of their sexual lives. A giant pair of lizards, Leslie and Sarah, on the cusp of making the evolutionary step from water to land, emerge from the ocean. At first, understandably, there is mutual distrust, especially between the two males. The lizard couple does not comprehend the concept of emotions or the complexities of human life. Charlie and Nancy do their best to explain about family, technology, love, and death. When Charlie makes Sarah cry by asking what she would do if Leslie went away and never returned, thus causing her to feel sorrow for the first time, her mate responds with fury, and they decide to return to the ocean — to not evolve. Nancy begs them to stay, since they will, after all, eventually return (such is the power of evolution). She, and to a lesser extent Charlie, offer to help. The last line of the play is Leslie's "Begin."

In a 2003 interview with Stephen Bottoms in *The Cambridge Companion to Edward Albee*, Albee commented on the significance of this last line: "It's a threat. . . . They're going back under the water because it's too awful up here, and they're learning things like loss and crying and death, which they'd never known. So they're wanting to go back home, even though they can't. And Charlie and Nancy say, 'no, please wait, we can help you.' And Leslie turns around and says, 'OK buddy, begin.' Meaning, 'and if you don't succeed, I'll rip you to pieces.' That's the whole intention of that last line. If you misunderstand that, then it's a misunderstanding of the play as profound as many misunderstandings of *Our Town*."

For the first time, Albee himself directed the premiere. The play went through a number of readings and subsequent revisions. Between the first and second day of rehearsal for the premiere, the play (which was originally three acts) was radically cut when the playwright excised the second act, which took place underwater in the lizard couple's world. Albee has noted that the uncut version was as long as Wagner's *Parsifal*, although funnier. It opened at the Shubert Theater on Broadway on January 26, 1975, to mixed reviews. It closed after sixty-five performances. This time it was Clive Barnes in *The New York Times* (January 27, 1975) who championed Albee, calling *Seascape* a "major dramatic event." It was awarded the Elizabeth Hull–Kate Warriner Award by the Dramatists Guild Council (the 1974–75 season's best play dealing with controversial political, religious, or social issues) and snagged Albee his second Pulitzer Prize.

GOLDEN BOY NO MORE

Critical response to Albee became increasingly hostile, and audiences did not respond well to the plays that followed *Seascape*. In a sense, Albee was sent into critical exile; it would not be until the 90s that he would again enjoy a commercial success, although this did not stop Albee from continuing to put his writings out there. He has often noted that there is a disconnect between popularity and excellence.

Listening (A Chamber Play) and *Counting the Ways (A Vaudeville)* were meant to be companion pieces, and both premiered in London in 1976, however, not together. The former was performed on the radio and the latter at the National Theatre.

In *Listening*, The Girl (a schizophrenic), The Man (a cook), and The Woman (apparently a therapist) statically encounter one another in what appears to be the garden of an asylum. Periodically a recorded voice intones the number of each scene, concluding the play with "End." The idea of being truly heard is at the center of this appropriately named play. The Girl repeatedly accuses The Woman of not paying attention to her. After The Woman relates the story of a suicide, The Girl displays her own slit wrists, demonstrating that she, at least, has been listening. The title of *Counting the Ways* comes from an Elizabeth Barrett Browning poem. In a series of twenty-one scenes that each end in a blackout, He and She talk about love. In a Brechtian touch, a sign is lowered on stage with the name of the play; later another sign instructs the actors to introduce themselves to the audience. The play deals with, as He says, a "slow falling apart," of separate beds, loss of love, and resulting pain. Bigsby observed: "His characters are left stranded without plot, drained of personal histories, denied complexity, severed from ambiguity, without passion. Language has detached itself from function." Neither play was well received.

His next play, *The Lady from Dubuque*, had its Broadway premiere in 1980. Both audience and critics were confused. It had been inspired by Elisabeth Kübler-Ross's *On Death and Dying*. Albee's producer, Richard Barr, closed it after twelve performances. Albee was enraged. He later admitted that he had not been sober enough to do the needed revisions. Despair seems to be at the center of this dark work. As Bigsby noted: "Albee continues to warn the world against a fate which he apparently no longer sees any way of avoiding." He goes on to observe that the "petty betrayals, the denials of friendship and the refusal to grant reality to death, create a logic which slowly unwinds in what is in effect another litany of human betrayal, another requiem for the lost liberal dream of a morally responsive self, for a world poisoned at source by self-interest and fear. The characters announce their love for one another only to deny it by their actions. The empty games and bitter arguments, as in so many of his earlier plays, are a substitute for genuine contact." However, David Richards in a *New York Times* article quotes Joanna Steichen, Albee's close friend who is a psychotherapist. She observed, "Edward sees and reports deep-down emotional truths so accurately that it's just too painful for some people. *Lady from Dubuque* was the only honest cancer play at a time when there was a spate of cancer plays in which the characters behaved as saints or martyrs. In Edward's play, they behaved as people, with manic self-interest and fear and selfish need."

Broadway saw another Albee opening in 1981, an adaptation of Vladimir Nabokov's *Lolita*. It seems to have been an unpleasant experience from beginning to end. In preparation of the script, there were intense conflicts with the producer, Jerry Sherlock, and the Nabokov estate (who objected to Albee's creation of a narrator who was too closely identified as depicting Nabokov himself). Donald Sutherland played Humbert Humbert. Unhappy with Albee's writing, he tried to insert pages from the novel and would cut his lines as he saw fit. In addition, money was an issue, and production values were cut: The dreary sets creaked during the scene changes, and lower-watt bulbs were used in the lighting instruments to save money. The script was so long that Albee wanted it to be performed over two nights. Eventually, the producer forced Albee to scale it back to the length of a single evening's performance (at a time when his drinking was interfering with his writing ability). Albee always maintained that the best version was the longer one. It opened in Boston in January 1981 to mixed reviews, and early audiences were offended. This offense apparently led to record attendance at the Wilbur Theater the two weeks it played Boston. The production returned to New York ostensibly to prepare for its opening there, but the director was off on another job, and Albee had left on a lecture tour. Nevertheless, the play opened on March 19, 1981, with a delayed curtain due to picketing by Women Against Pornography. It received wretched reviews and closed nine days later.

Ironically, *Lolita* became Albee's second-greatest moneymaker after *Who's Afraid of Virginia Woolf?* It was later sold for film rights, and Albee shared the million-dollar sale with the Nabokov estate.

But the play that would send Albee away from Broadway for thirteen years is a play that he still feels has not been given a chance to succeed, *The Man Who Had Three Arms*. In this play, a man, called Himself, achieves sudden fame and adoration when he grows a third arm, but he then is rejected when that arm withers away. Albee wrote the play in Miami for the New World Festival of the Arts. Away from the caring eyes of Jonathan Thomas, he was drinking again. It opened there in 1982 at the Coconut Grove Playhouse, was revised and played in Chicago's Goodman Theater, then went on to Broadway's Lyceum Theatre in 1983. The critics, who saw it as a personal attack on those who had failed to appreciate Albee's recent endeavors, ripped it to shreds. Frank Rich of *The New York Times* was typical: "But whoever Himself is — whether a one-time freak or a playwright in mid-career crisis — his beefs with the world are shrill and unmoving, no matter how much the author tries to inflate them into an indictment of 'the American dream.'" It closed after sixteen performances.

KEEP ON KEEPING ON

Following the critical pileup of *Lady*, *Lolita*, and *Three Arms*, Albee turned to the world of academia, which eagerly welcomed him with open arms. He conducted writer's workshops, mentored new playwrights, wrote and premiered new works, directed plays, spoke out on political issues, and accepted honorary degrees and other recognitions, including his 1985 induction into the Theater Hall of Fame in the Gershwin Theater in New York City. It was also during this period that he gained control over his alcoholism, with the help of Jonathan Thomas and a diagnosis of diabetes.

Among other appointments, Albee was named a Distinguished Professor of Drama at the University of Houston in 1988, where he taught an annual playwriting class until 2003. He was named an Alley Associate Artist by the Alley Theater in Houston in 1989 and directed both his and others' works there. He hit the lecture circuit as well, where he loved to point out the other playwrights whose plays were not being performed on Broadway: Sophocles, Aristophanes, Shakespeare, Marlow, Molière, Ibsen, Chekhov, Pirandello, Beckett, and Genet.

As an outspoken member of PEN, ITI, and the Dramatists Guild, Albee's fame allowed him to be very influential for causes about which he felt strongly. With such other literary luminaries as Arthur Miller and Harold Pinter, he spoke out against censorship and upheld the rights of dissident artists. In 1985, he brought his production of Sam Shepard's *Hawk Moon* to the Czech Theater Institute. Over the objection of the local authorities, he managed to get several dissident artists, including Václav Havel, into the production and to the after-show dinner at the U.S. Embassy. Albee took every opportunity to speak out and up for the beleaguered. He argued that art should be a catalyst for change and that art is viewed as dangerous by some governments because art has the capacity to show up shortcomings and inspire us to live differently and more fully.

Albee directed many productions of his own works during this period (including several of his premieres) at UC-Irvine, the University of Houston, the English Theatre in Vienna, the Alley Theater in Houston, and the Ensemble Theatre in Cincinnati. Among the premieres was *Marriage Play* in 1985, about a long-time married couple struggling to not be married anymore. In 1992 he directed the premiere of *The Lorca Play* (about the Spanish playwright, who was a martyr to Fascism). Also he directed the premiere of his own *Fragments: A Sit Around*, a script structured to play like music as stories accumulate, one upon the next. Four men and four women read proverbs aloud, prompting tales about their past or contemplating life's mysteries. In so doing, they try to make genuine human connection (a leitmotif seen throughout Albee's works).

DEATH COMES CALLING

Albee experienced several deaths during this period. Links to his glory days were severed when his long-time director, Alan Schneider, died in 1984 when he was struck down by a motorcycle in London. The same year, William Ritman, a frequent set designer for Albee, died of cancer. In 1987, the poet Howard Moss, a dear friend, died of heart failure. In 1989, Richard Barr, who as Albee's producer had championed him for three decades, died from liver failure associated with HIV infection. Profound grief resulted from the deaths of Moss and Barr, not so the other death in 1989, that of his mother.

Frankie's memory had begun to fail. In 1988, her physical condition worsened, and she grew ever frailer. In 1989 she succumbed to pneumonia at the age of ninety-two. Albee rushed to the hospital, but did not arrive in time; Frankie was already gone. Albee arranged for her funeral, which was attended by local friends. Albee was the only relative present. After initially leaving Albee the bulk of her estate in 1984, Frankie changed her will in 1986 to leave him only a minimum bequest. This occurred after a mutual friend told Frankie that she and

Albee would have a better relationship if she would only accept the fact that he was gay. This kindly gesture appears to have backfired badly. According to his biographer, Albee felt that his mother had dis-inherited him a second time, as she had forty years before when he had stormed out of her life. Had their over-twenty-year reconciliation meant nothing?

Ironically, or perhaps appropriately, her death gave Albee the play that would bring him back to New York City stages and critical acclaim.

THE COMEBACK KID

Just about a year after his mother died, Albee began writing a play, *Three Tall Women*. When it opened in New York City in 1994 at the Off-Broadway Vineyard Theatre, it gave the former *enfant terrible* the experience of being a sixty-six-year-old comeback kid. It would also gain Albee his third Pulitzer Prize.

In a 1994 essay on the play in *Stretching My Mind*, he claimed he had been writing it his whole life, from his earliest memory of his adoptive mother (her looking on as he was held as an infant in his nanny's arms) to Frankie's death over sixty years later. It is a play Albee freely admits is autobiographical. It also proved to be cathartic. While discussing *Three Tall Women* in an interview with Stephen Bottoms in *The Cambridge Companion*, Albee observed of his mother: "I had a rather grudging admiration for her survivability. We never got along, ever, and I used to think it was all her fault. But I think I was probably not a very easy kid, and I don't think it was any willfulness on her part to be awful. I just don't think she knew how to be a parent."

There are three characters: A, an old woman; B, a middle-aged woman; and C, a young woman. In Act One, C is a lawyer helping her client, A, sort out her finances. A is physically fading and a bit senile. B is the old woman's paid caretaker. A prods and verbally pokes the other two women as her entire life is laid out for examination, including her passionless marriage and the son who left home. Like Frankie, she turns on a dime from being gracious, to vicious, to pitiful. While recounting a horrible memory, she suffers a stroke. Act Two reveals what appears to be A's comatose body in bed, with B and C in attendance. But then A enters, alive and far more lucid then she was in Act One. The three tall women are now A at the three stages of her life: imperious dowager, stately matron, and young woman. Her estranged son enters and crosses silently to her bedside, looking down at the body as A, B, and C discuss him, each from the perspective of her age and memory. They discuss and examine the different stages of her life, at last coming to an understanding of who and why she is and was.

Like *The Zoo Story*, his first major success, *Three Tall Women* opened in Europe, at the English Theatre in Vienna. It was accepted for production with only the first act written. As this act went into rehearsals, Albee began writing the second act in his hotel room. In a Pirandello-esque development, another character appeared, the prodigal son. It opened on June 14, 1991 and received polite reviews. However, friends and admirers of Albee sensed that this play was significant.

Three Tall Women entered the United States under the radar. No one in New York was interested in producing Albee. He was considered a great playwright of the past. But Lawrence Sacharow, the artistic director of the River Arts Repertory in Woodstock, New York, convinced Albee to let him direct the American premiere at his theater. When the play opened on July 30, 1992, it received enthusiastic local reviews, sold out its run, and was extended. Word of mouth carried the news to New York City and interest began to grow, but no transfer to New York City was immediately forthcoming. Albee remained loyal to this particular production, its director, and cast. Finally Douglas Aibel, the artistic director of the Off-Broadway Vineyard Theatre, scheduled it for a January 1994 opening.

Uncommon for Albee, it received nearly unanimously glowing reviews; even some of his worst detractors praised *Three Tall Women*. It moved to the larger Off-Broadway Promenade Theater and ran until

August 1995, enjoying a stunning, sold-out success — only *Who's Afraid of Virginia Woolf?* had had a longer run. In addition to his third Pulitzer, it won the New York Drama Critics' Circle Award. Albee received the Obie for Sustained Achievement in Theater.

During this same period, the Signature Theatre Company in New York City also honored Albee. Signature dedicates the entirety of each season to a single American playwright. For their 1993–94 season, that playwright was Edward Albee. He confessed to Carol Rocamora in an interview in the January 2008 *American Theatre*, "That season reminded me I was alive." This "Albee Season" opened with the New York premieres of *Marriage Play, Counting the Ways,* and *Listening,* followed by his "sand plays": *Box, The Sandbox,* and *Finding the Sun. Fragments* closed the season.

Marking Albee's return to Broadway, *A Delicate Balance* was given a critically acclaimed revival, with Gerald Gutierrez directing. It opened at the Plymouth Theater on April 21, 1996. Rosemary Harris, who played Agnes, having seen *Three Tall Women,* brought much of her understanding of Albee's mother into her role. It received laudatory reviews and won the Tony for best revival.

An Albee revival was well on its way.

PASSAGES

Sadly, this hallmark year also saw the death of Albee's oldest childhood friend, Noel Farrand, who died of complications from diabetes, alcohol, and cigarettes on August 21, 1996. Farrand would have been thrilled to see his old friend, only a few months later, being feted at the Kennedy Center Honors for lifetime contributions to the nation's culture. In December of 1996, Albee received the National Medal of Arts from President Clinton. Ever the activist, Albee took the opportunity to speak out and up to the president on behalf of the beleaguered National Endowment for the Arts. At a reception before the event, President Clinton said of Albee: "Tonight our nation — born in rebellion — pays tribute to you, Edward Albee. In your rebellion, the American theater was reborn."

Albee sat with his beloved partner, Jonathan Thomas, in one of the high box seats for the evening's tributes. The next morning *The Washington Post* mistakenly captioned a picture of John Steinbeck's widow and Albee as "Playwright Edward Albee and his wife, Percy, take center stage last night at the Kennedy Center." Vastly amused, according to Albee's biographer, Albee called Elaine Steinbeck and offered a divorce. He then wrote a correction to the newspaper: "While I was delighted that *The Post* photographed me at the Kennedy Center, I was shocked that the newspaper had given me a wife, and that her name is Percy. This kind of sloppy journalism is deeply distressing, for two people are with me in the photograph: Mrs. John Steinbeck — widow of the Nobel laureate, who is a dear friend, though to whom I am not married and whose name is not Percy — and Mr. Jonathan Thomas, with whom I have been living happily for 27 years."

OH BABY

Albee's next work, *The Play About the Baby*, premiered at the Almeida Theater in London on September 1, 1998. Both funny and sinister, it opens with Girl, who is hugely pregnant, rushing offstage. Boy follows. After some moaning and screaming, a slap is heard, followed by a baby's cry. They return to the stage with their bundle of joy wrapped in a blanket. After feeding the baby, the Boy wants in on the action too, so Girl drops the baby off offstage and returns, offering her breast to Boy. They chase each other around the stage in pre-Fall, Edenic bliss, until the ominous arrival of Man and Woman, an older couple. With vaudeville turns, Man and Woman share random thoughts and stories, periodically addressing the audience, as when Man barks at the audience, "Pay attention to this. What's true and what isn't is a tricky business, no?" They tease and teach the young, amorous couple about how dangerous the world really is, and the tone gradually changes to one of threat. At the end of Act One, Man announces, "We've come to take the baby." In Act Two, Man and Woman continue their comic riffs, as when Woman renders Man's musings in sign language. The threat of baby-snatching builds. At the conclusion, Man lifts the blanketed baby into the air, and with "Ladies and Gentlemen! See what we have here! The baby bundle," he tosses it above his head; the blanket unfurls and comes down empty. The mood darkens when the Man and Woman try to convince Boy and Girl that the baby never existed. There is no resolution; the question of the baby's fate is never answered.

It made its way to America by way of the Alley Theater in Houston in 2000 under Albee's direction, finally making it to New York City in February 2001 at the Century Center for the Performing Arts under the direction of David Esbjornson.

Reviews were mixed, of course, some thinking the play was derivative of Albee's earlier works (perhaps most obviously, the idea of the missing/absent child). Others thought that Albee's long-standing leitmotifs were being explored in a new and startling style. Ben Brantley of *The New York Times* (February 2, 2001) observed: "Mr. Albee's gaze has always focused on the abyss. *Baby* is about nothing less than being forced to acknowledge its existence. The Boy . . . repeatedly asks that he be allowed to dwell in innocence for just a bit longer, to let the 'pain and loss' come later. 'Give us some time,' he begs. The Man's summary answer: 'Time's up.'"

Tragically ironic, time was also up for America's innocence. A few months after *The Play About the Baby*'s New York City premiere, on September 11, 2001, Albee saw the plane hit the second World Trade Center and the collapse of the towers. He packed a suitcase with scripts and medicines and walked the fifty blocks uptown to Penn Station and took a train to his home in Montauk.

SHOCKING BROADWAY AGAIN

Appropriately in an America that was to become increasingly intolerant, his next play would deal with what Albee called in "About This Goat," a 2004 essay in *Stretching My Mind:* "the limits of our tolerance of the behavior of others than ourselves, especially when such behavior ran counter to what we believed to be acceptable social and moral boundaries. . . ." *The Goat, or Who Is Sylvia?* was the first new play by Albee to premiere on Broadway since 1983. Opening at the Golden Theater in March 2002, it won the Tony Award for best play and the New York Drama Critics' Circle Award, among others.

If the theater community had been taken aback by the profanity in *Who's Afraid of Virginia Woolf?*, Albee proved that he could still shock and provoke spirited debate. As with his vitriolic and funny play about George and Martha, audience members walked out, and critics were unsure how to respond. But like *Woolf*, word of mouth resulted in increased audiences and enthusiasm for the play.

Its secondary title, *Who Is Sylvia?*, is taken from a song in Shakespeare's *The Two Gentleman of Verona* (a comedy about love and its betrayal). Ben Brantley observed that *The Goat* seems to open in the comic world of Neil Simon. But while the comedy continues, the humor becomes more startled and uncomfortable, and eventually the comic elements die away all together. The world is definitely Albee's, and the subject is a love that dare not speak its name.

Like many of Albee's plays, its setting is a living room of a middle-aged married couple. In contrast to Albee's other married couples, Martin, a wildly successful architect, and his wife, Stevie, seem to have a nearly idyllic marriage. They even get along with their seventeen-year-old gay son (their kid), whose name is Billy. But it is not his sexual orientation that dare not speak its name, although the acceptance of their gay son does provide a contrast for a love that dares not. Albee chooses to reveal the forbidden love quite early in the play: "*in a greatly exaggerated Noel Coward manner*," the couple joke about the idea that Martin is having an affair, with Martin proclaiming his true love, "She's a goat; Sylvia is a goat!" Stevie chortles at the seeming joke and exits. Martin laments, "You try to *tell* them, you try to be *honest*. What do they do? They laugh at you." Again, issues of the inadequacies of language and the difficulties of truly connecting to another human are at the center of this script. For Martin has indeed fallen in love with a goat and is having an affair. Martin reveals this to his oldest and best friend, Ross, who is appalled: "THIS IS A GOAT! YOU'RE HAVING AN AFFAIR WITH A GOAT! YOU'RE FUCKING A GOAT!" In the next scene, the hysterical Billy is confronting his father, who argues that his son should accept Sylvia the way he accepts his son's sexual partners. Stevie, who has been informed of Martin's farmyard dalliance by Ross, cannot comprehend that her husband still loves her: "How can you love me when you love so much less?" She goes on to explain that while one prepares "for the jolts along the way, disturbances of the peace, the lies, the evasions, the infidelities . . ." one does not prepare for something that happens "outside the rules, that doesn't relate to The Way The Game Is Played." And as many people must have felt a half a year after the World Trade Center Towers fell, she declares, "I want the whole day to rewind — start over. I want the reel to reverse." As the façade of their perfect life literally falls in pieces around them (as Stevie calmly shatters their possessions), Martin tries to explain that he and Sylvia have a connection beyond language, "an understanding so natural, so intense that I will *never* forget it, as intense as the night you and I finally came at the same time." Stevie, having been reduced to nothing, leaves, threatening to bring him down with her. The final scene takes the question of acceptance even further, as Billy and his father start to clean up the mess. Billy, caught between between rage and love, begins crying and kissing his father, culminating in the following: "*Then it turns — or does it? — and he kisses Martin full on the mouth — a deep, sobbing, sexual kiss.*" Ross, having entered just in time for the kiss, prompts the defensive Martin to explore the issues of sexual boundaries, relating the time when a "friend" (clearly himself) got an erection while bouncing his baby son (clearly Billy) in his lap. Martin exclaims, "Is there anything 'we people' don't get off on? . . . Remember Saint Sebastian with all the arrows shot into him? He probably came! God knows the faithful did! Shall I go on!? You want to hear about the cross!?" It is Ross, Martin maintains, who has done the unnatural, by informing Stevie and destroying her life. The sound of the front door is heard, and death joins love. Stevie enters, covered with blood, and dragging a dead goat, Sylvia, her throat slashed. In anguish, Martin asks, "What did she ever do?" Sylvia's response, "She loved you . . . you say. As much as *I* do."

The Goat, or Who Is Sylvia? is not a play about bestiality, although there is the goat. It is not a comedy, although Albee's razor-sharp witticisms are liberally represented in the dialogue. While it does not appear in all of its published editions, there is an parenthetical subheading: "(Notes Toward a Definition of Tragedy)." It is worth remembering that "goat song" was what the ancient Greeks called tragedy.

"I CAN'T GO ON, I'LL GO ON"

This renowned quotation from Samuel Beckett, one of Albee's major influences, has been echoed by Albee himself on numerous occasions. In the year 2003, it surely became his credo. His beloved partner and helpmeet, Jonathan Thomas, was diagnosed with bladder cancer. There was an operation and chemotherapy. Albee set everything aside to care for his partner.

On May 2, 2005, Jonathan Thomas lost the battle and died at fifty-nine. Albee, frozen in grief, did not write or direct for some time. In a 2007 article in *The New York Times* by Jesse Green, Albee stated that their expectation was that Thomas would take care of Albee, who was eighteen years older, "But life doesn't work out the way it's supposed to. . . . The mourning never ends; it just changes. . . . we had such a good, long relationship: nearly thirty-five years. That's a long time, a life in itself. Of course that makes it worse, but at the same time you can't just say, 'How dare you go away from me?' — which is an attitude a lot of people get. 'How dare you die!' There's got to be a lot of 'Thank you' too. 'Thank you for being alive and being with me for so long.'"

A month after Thomas's death, Albee had to "go on." At the June 2005 Tony Awards, Edward Albee received the Lifetime Achievement Tony Award (the only other playwright to have received that honor was Arthur Miller).

GOING BACK TO THE ZOO

It would not be until 2007 that another Albee play would open in New York (having had its premiere in 2004 at the Hartford Stage Company). It received glowing reviews. *Peter and Jerry* is a full-length play that uses *The Zoo Story* as its second act. Having long thought that the character of Peter needed more explanation, Albee wrote a first act, *Homelife*, which takes place in the home of Peter and his wife. In his review of the New York production, Ben Brantley in *The New York Times* (November 12, 2007) described it as "a canny, self-contained chamber play about marriage, a consideration, both sober and funny, of the loneliness within a shared life. . . . Peter and Ann are as articulate as the romantic sparring partners of Noel Coward plays. But it becomes clear that genuine communication doesn't come easily to them. . . . 'We should talk,' says Ann, in the line that opens *Homelife*. That Peter, immersed in a book, doesn't hear her is a joke typical of Albee who knows how very little people really listen." In comparing it to *The Zoo Story*, Brantley offers Albee high praise: "There are telling differences in inflection and timber [sic] between these creations of a man in his twenties and his seventies. But there is no mistaking that they are products of one enduring and consistent voice, a voice unparalleled in American theater for its surgical elegance in exploring the animal in humanity."

HAPPY BIRTHDAY, MR. ALBEE

In 2008, Edward Albee turned eighty years old, and it seemed as if the theatrical world was celebrating his life. There were productions of Albee scripts, Albee himself directing *The American Dream* and *The Sandbox* at the Cherry Lane Theater in New York City (opening in March, shortly after his birthday), and revivals taking place all over.

After setting it aside five years before to care for Thomas, Albee completed *Me, Myself, and I*. It premiered at the McCarter Theater in Princeton, New Jersey, in January. Employing Albee's sardonic humor, this dark comedy is about identical twins named otto and OTTO. Mother can't tell her sons apart. The confusion increases when OTTO announces that he's leaving home (to become Chinese) and that otto no longer exists. Word games abound in this play, with, appropriately, an abundance of double meanings. Ben Brantley in his *Times* review (January 28, 2008) observed, "It feels as if every musty and trusty convention in theater is at some point exhumed. Greek tragedy, comedy according to Shakespeare and Molière, the heady experimentation of Pirandello and Ionesco: they're all summoned and discarded happily and brazenly. So are the devices of the lyrical narrator à la Tennessee Williams and the spot-lighted soliloquy." On the McCarter Theater's Web site, the director Emily Mann described it as "a very funny story of a pair of twin brothers and their family, but on a deeper level the play addresses core questions of our modern society. How do we shape our identities and sense of self in a world that seems to inscribe culture upon us? . . . In an age of molecular biology, how do we distinguish ourselves from our DNA? What is the meaning of family in a fractured world? And what does it mean to define oneself as an American? *Me, Myself, and I* examines key themes that have become central to Albee's work: the idealization of the absent parent; the way we construct families; and the fine line between imagination and reality."

The same year, Edward Albee's *Occupant* (having closed during 2002 previews because of the illness of its star, Anne Bancroft) received its premiere at the Signature Theater Company in May with Mercedes

Ruehl playing Louise Nevelson, the abstract expressionist sculptor who died in 1988. Albee had interviewed Nevelson for a catalogue to accompany one of her showings. In an interview with Carol Rocamora in *American Theatre*, Albee observed that he "soon came to be one of her 'familiars,' had dinner with her from time to time at her place and got to like her very much. She seemed to like me, too, and what I wrote about her. She once said she was convinced that every piece of sculpture is part of one large sculpture. I, in turn, suspect that every play I write is part of one large play. Everything I feel about her is right there in *Occupant*." The play has two characters, the deceased Louise Nevelson, and Man, who is interviewing her. When she asks if he is nervous, he responds, "A little. I've never interviewed someone who is dead before." Brantley of the *Times* observes in a June 6, 2008, review that the heat of the play is about the nature of artistry itself, "But what concerns Mr. Albee in bringing his friend back to life is the issue of what allows an artist — unavoidably an outsider — to persevere until she becomes what she always, on some level, intended to be. This necessarily lonely process of self-fulfillment is what gives *Occupant* an emotional heft beyond that of a mere biographical sketch."

ALBEE'S LEGACY

Through his writing, his activism, his directing, and his teaching, Edward Albee has given an inestimable gift to the world. Splitting time between his art-filled loft in Tribeca (paintings by Chagall, Kandinsky, Arp, sculpture by Nevelson, and figures from Africa) and his seaside home in Montauk, Albee continues to pursue the only life he could ever have lived, the life of the artist. It seems appropriate to let Albee himself have the last word.

In an interview with David Richards of *The New York Times*, June 16, 1991, Albee maintained, "All my plays are about people missing the boat, closing down too young, coming to the end of their lives with regret at things not done, as opposed to things done. I find that most people spend too much time living as if they're never going to die. They skid through their lives. Sleep through them sometimes. Anyway, there are only two things to write about — life and death." More recently, in a 2007 *Times* article by Jesse Green, Albee commented on his future artistic life, "I'm not in a hurry. I keep having ideas. The creative mind doesn't seem to have collapsed. I'll worry more about that when I'm ninety. Meanwhile I take pretty good care of myself, and I have no enthusiasm whatever about dying. I think it's a terrible waste of time, and I don't want to participate in it."

SUGGESTED EXCERPTS

from Albee's Plays

IN AN HOUR BOOKS, LLC regrets the absence of representative excerpts from the plays of Edward Albee, who, through his agent, declined to permit the use of any portion of his plays to be published in this volume.

We respectfully submit that this permissions policy does not reflect the public interest aspect of U.S. Copyright law. In our view the Albee policy in effect extends the protection of the Proprietor beyond what the copyright law intends. Whereas the copyright laws protect the creator's right to exploit the property, the laws also intend that the property be made available for uses that would serve and protect the public interest in the property. It is our view that copyright use policies such as this will serve the interests of those who are working to dilute copyright protection for the creators.

A guide to accessing the selected excerpts appears in the pages which follows.

These excerpt suggestions are from the playwright's major plays. They are meant to give a taste of the playwright's work. Each short introduction helps the reader identify the excerpt within the play. The suggested excerpts, which are in chronological order, illustrate the main themes mentioned in the In an Hour essay. Premiere dates are provided.

from **The Zoo Story** (1959)

CHARACTERS

Peter
Jerry

Near the end of this one-act, the excerpt begins as Peter declares that he's put up with Jerry long enough, and Jerry tries to push Peter off of the bench. The excerpt and play reaches its horrifying conclusion with Jerry's death.

from **The American Dream** (1961)

CHARACTERS

Grandma
Young Man
Mommy
Daddy
Mrs. Barker

In the closing minutes of the play, the excerpt begins as Grandma, alone on the stage, looks around and says good-bye to her home, and the Young Man enters and sees her out. The excerpt and play concludes as Mommy and Daddy at last gain a satisfactory "son" after the dreadful disappointment of their first "bumble of joy," and Grandma bids the audience farewell.

from **Who's Afraid of Virginia Woolf?** (1962)

ACT THREE

CHARACTERS

George
Martha
Nick
Honey

From Act Three, near the conclusion, George and Martha, after a night of drinking and "games" with Nick and Honey, have only one more game to play, dealing with a son who exists only as a vital fantasy. The excerpt begins as George tells Martha that a Western Union messenger has delivered a telegram with some bad news. The excerpt concludes with Martha crying that she did not mean to break the rules of their game; she did forgot and mention their "son," but that George did not have to kill him.

from **A Delicate Balance** (1967)

ACT ONE

CHARACTERS

> Agnes
> Tobias
> Edna
> Harry
> Claire

Near the end of Act One, the excerpt begins as Agnes and Tobias let their terrified friends, Edna and Harry, into their proper, upper-middle-class home. The excerpt concludes at the end of Act One as Agnes leads Edna and Harry upstairs, and Claire enigmatically declares to Tobias that something has begun.

from **Three Tall Women** (1991)

ACT TWO

CHARACTERS

A
B
C

Midway into Act Two, the "three tall women," A, B, and C — reflecting Albee's mother at three stages of her life — discuss her family and her past from the perspective of youth, middle age, and old age. The excerpt begins as B declares how the family cried when her father died and concludes as A, B, and C discuss the son who has returned, and A observes to her younger selves that while she never forgave him, she did want him to return.

THE READING ROOM

YOUNG ACTORS AND THEIR TEACHERS

Bigsby, C. W. E. "Edward Albee." In *A Critical Introduction to Twentieth-Century American Drama*. Vol 2. New York: Cambridge University Press, 1984.

Bottoms, Stephen, ed. *The Cambridge Companion to Edward Albee*. Cambridge: Cambridge University Press, 2005.

Downer, Alan S., ed. "An Interview with Edward Albee." In *The American Theatre Today*. New York: Basic Books, 1967.

Goldman, Jeffrey. "An Interview with Edward Albee." *Studies in American Drama, 1945–Present* 6 (1991): 59–69.

Kolin, Philip C. *Conversations with Edward Albee*. Jackson: University Press of Mississippi, 1988.

Maslon, Laurence. "Edward Albee." In *The Playwright's Art: Conversations with Contemporary American Dramatists*. New Brunswick: Rutgers University Press, 1992.

McCarthy, Gerry. *Edward Albee*. New York: St. Martin's Press, 1987.

Parker, Dorothy, ed. *Essays on Modern American Drama: Williams, Miller, Albee, and Shepard*. Toronto: University of Toronto Press, 1987.

Roudané, Matthew C. "An Interview with Edward Albee." *Southern Humanities Review* 16 (1982): 29–44.

Roudané, Matthew C. "Albee on Albee." *RE: Artes Liberals* 10:2 (1984): 1–8.

Seldes, Marian. "Albee and Me." *American Theatre* 13 (Sept. 1996): 24–26.

Zinman, Toby. *Edward Albee*. Michigan Modern Dramatists. Ann Arbor: University of Michigan Press, 2008.

This extensive bibliography lists books about the playwright according to whom the books might be of interest. If you would like to research further something that interests you in the text, lists of references, sources cited, and editions used in this book are found in this section.

SCHOLARS, STUDENTS, PROFESSORS

Amacher, Richard E. *Edward Albee*. Revised edition. New York: Twayne Publishers, 1982.

_____ and Margaret Rule. *Edward Albee at Home and Abroad: A Bibliography*. New York: Twayne Publishers, 1969.

Bigsby, C.W.E. *Albee*. Edinburgh: Oliver and Boyd, 1969.

_____. *Edward Albee: Bibliography, Biography, Playography (Theatre Checklist 22)*. London: TQ Publications, 1980.

_____, ed. *Edward Albee: A Collection of Critical Essays*. Englewood Cliffs, N.J.: Prentice-Hall, 1975.

Bloom, Harold, ed. *Edward Albee: Modern Critical Views*. New York: Chelsea House, 1987.

Cohn, Ruby. *Edward Albee*. Minneapolis: University of Minnesota Press, 1969.

De La Fuente, Patricia, et al. (eds.). *Edward Albee: Planned Wilderness: Interview, Essays, and Bibliography*. Edinburgh, Tex.: Pan American University Press, 1980.

Debusscher, Gilbert. *Edward Albee: Tradition and Renewal*. Translated by Anne D. Williams. Brussels: American Studies Center, 1967.

Giantvalley, Scott. *Edward Albee: A Reference Guide*. Boston: G. K. Hall, 1987.

Green, Charles Lee. *Edward Albee: An Annotated Bibliography, 1968–1977*. New York: AMS Press, 1980.

Hayman, Ronald. *Edward Albee*. New York: Frederick Ungar Publishing, 1973.

Hirsch, Foster. *Who's Afraid of Edward Albee*. Berkeley: Creative Arts, 1978.

Kerjan, Liliane. *Le Théâtre d'Edward Albee*. Paris: Klincksieck, 1978.

Kolin, Philip C., and J. Madison Davis, eds. *Critical Essays on Edward Albee*. Boston: G. K. Hall, 1986.

Mann, Bruce J., ed. *Edward Albee: A Casebook*. New York: Routledge, 2003.

Mayberry, Bob. *Theatre of Discord: Dissonance in Beckett, Albee and Pinter*. Rutherford, N.J.: Farleigh Dickinson University Press, 1989.

Paolucci, Anne. *From Tension to Tonic: The Plays of Edward Albee*. Carbondale: Southern Illinois University Press, 1972.

Roudané, Matthew C. "Edward Albee." In *American Playwrights Since 1945: A Guide to Scholarship, Criticism, and Performance.* Edited by Philip C. Kolin. Westport, Conn.: Greenwood Press, 1989.

Schultz-Seitz, Ruth Eva. *Edward Albee, der Dichterphilosoph der Buhne.* Frankfurt am Main: Vittorio Klostermann, 1966.

Tyce, Richard. *Edward Albee: A Bibliography.* Metuchen, N.J.: Scarecrow Press, 1986.

Vos, Nelvin. *Eugene Ionesco and Edward Albee: A Critical Essay.* Grand Rapids, Mich.: W. B. Eerdmans, 1968.

Wasserman, Julian N., et al., eds. *Edward Albee: An Interview and Essays.* Houston: University of St. Thomas Press, 1983.

THEATERS, PRODUCERS

Braem, Helmut M. *Edward Albee.* Revised edition. Hannover, Germany: Velber Verlag, 1977.

Horn, Barbara Lee. *Edward Albee: A Research and Production Sourcebook (Modern Dramatists Research and Production Sourcebooks).* Westport, Conn.: Praeger Publishers, 2003.

Roudané, Matthew C. *Understanding Edward Albee.* Columbia: University of South Carolina Press, 1987.

Rutenberg, Michael E. *Edward Albee: Playwright in Protest.* New York: Drama Book Specialists, 1969.

ACTORS, DIRECTORS, THEATER PROFESSIONALS

Bottoms, Stephen. *Albee: Who's Afraid of Virginia Woolf?* Cambridge: Cambridge University Press, 2000.

Flanagan, William. "Albee in the Village." *New York Herald Tribune* (27 Oct. 1963): 27.

Gussow, Mel. *Edward Albee: A Singular Journey.* New York: Simon and Schuster, 1999.

Roudané, Matthew C. *Who's Afraid of Virginia Woolf?: Necessary Fictions, Terrifying Realities.* Boston: Twayne Publishers, 1990.

Stenz, Anita Maria. *Edward Albee: The Poet of Loss.* The Hague: Mouton Publishers, 1978.

EDITIONS OF ALBEE'S WORKS USED FOR THIS BOOK

Albee, Edward. *Collected Plays of Edward Albee: 1958–1965*. Vol. 1. New York: Overlook, 2004.

_____. *Collected Plays of Edward Albee: 1966–1977*. Vol. 2. New York: Overlook, 2004.

_____. *Stretching My Mind: The Collected Essays 1960–2005*. New York: Carroll and Graf, 2005.

_____. *Collected Plays of Edward Albee: 1978–2003*. Vol. 3. New York: Overlook, 2006.

SOURCES CITED IN THIS BOOK

Amacher, Richard E. *Edward Albee*. Revised edition. New York: Twayne Publishers, 1982.

Barnes, Clive. "Albee's *Seascape* Is a Major Event." *New York Times*. (27 January 1975): 20.

Bigsby, C. W. E. "Edward Albee." In *A Critical Introduction to Twentieth-Century American Drama*. Vol 2. New York: Cambridge University Press, 1984.

Bottoms, Stephen. "Borrowed Time: An Interview with Edward Albee." In *The Cambridge Companion to Edward Albee*. Ed. Stephen Bottoms. Cambridge: Cambridge University Press, 2005.

Brantley, Ben. "Albee Laughing Dourly Ever After." *New York Times* (2 February 2001)

_____. "A Secret Paramour Who Nibbles." *New York Times* (11 March 2002).

_____. "Who's Afraid of the Menace Within? Not Edward Albee." *New York Times* (12 November 2007).

_____. "Resurrecting an Artist's Greatest Creation: Herself." *New York Times* (6 June 2008).

_____. "Ta-ta! Give 'Em the Old Existential Soft-Show." *New York Times*. (28 January 2008).

Clurman, Harold. "Albee on Balance." *New York Times* (13 November 1966).

_____. "Theatre." *Nation* 26 (25 March 1968): 420.

_____. "Theatre." *Nation* 212 (12 April 1971): 476–77

Edemariam, Aida. "Whistling in the Dark." *The Guardian* (10 January 2004) www.guardian.co.uk.

Esslin, Martin. *The Theatre of the Absurd.* New York: Anchor Books, 1961.

Green, Jesse. "Albee the Enigma, Now the Inescapable." *New York Times* (11 November 2007).

Gussow, Mel. *Edward Albee: A Singular Journey.* New York: Simon and Schuster, 1999.

Rich, Frank. "Stage: Drama by Albee, 'Man Who Had 3 Arms'." *New York Times* (6 April 1983).

Richards, David. "Edward Albee and the Road Not Taken." *New York Times* (16 June 1991).

Rocamora, Carol. "Albee Sizes Up the Dark Vast." In *American Theatre* 25:1 (January 2008): 30–33, 120–121.

Awards

"AND THE WINNER IS . . ."

	PULITZER PRIZE	TONY AWARD	NY DRAMA CRITICS CIRCLE AWARD		
			Best American	Best Foreign	Best Play
1957	Eugene O'Neill *Long Day's Journey Into Night*	Eugene O'Neill *Long Day's Journey Into Night*	Eugene O'Neill *Long Day's Journey Into Night*		
1958	Ketti Frings *Look Homeward, Angel*	Dore Schary *Sunrise at Campobello*	Ketti Frings *Look Homeward, Angel*		
1959	Archibald Macleish *J.B.*	Archibald Macleish *J.B.*	Lorraine Hansberry *A Raisin in the Sun*		
1960	Jerry Bock, music Sheldon Harnick, lyrics Jerome Wiedman, book George Abbott, book *Fiorello*	William Gibson *The Miracle Worker*	Lillian Hellman *Toys in the Attic*		
1961	Tad Mosel *All The Way Home*	Jean Anouilh *Beckett*	Tad Mosel *All the Way Home*		
1962	Frank Loesser and Abe Burrows *How to Succeed in Business Without Really Trying*	Robert Bolt *A Man for All Seasons*	Tennessee Williams *The Night of the Iguana*	Richard Bolt *A Man for All Seasons*	No Award
1963	No Award	**Edward Albee** ***Who's Afraid of Virginia Woolf?***	**Edward Albee** ***Who's Afraid of Virginia Woolf?***		
1964	No Award	John Osborne *Luther*	John Osborne *Luther*		
1965	Frank D. Gilroy *The Subject Was Roses*	Frank D. Gilroy *The Subject Was Roses*	Frank D. Gilroy *The Subject Was Roses*		
1966	No Award	Peter Weiss *Marat / Sade*	Peter Weiss *Marat / Sade*		

	PULITZER PRIZE	TONY AWARD	NY DRAMA CRITICS CIRCLE AWARD		
			Best American	Best Foreign	Best Play
1967	**Edward Albee** *A Delicate Balance*	Harold Pinter *The Homecoming*	Harold Pinter *The Homecoming*		
1968	No Award	Tom Stoppard *Rosencrantz and Guildenstern Are Dead*	Tom Stoppard *Rosencrantz and Guildenstern Are Dead*		
1969	Howard Sackler *The Great White Hope*	Howard Sackler *The Great White Hope*	Howard Sackler *The Great White Hope*		
1970	Charles Gordone *No Place to Be Somebody*	Frank McMahon *Borstal Boy*	Paul Zindel *The Effect of Gamma Rays on Man-In-The-Moon Marigolds*	No Award	Frank McMahon *Borstal Boy*
1971	Paul Zindel *The Effect of Gamma Rays on Man-In-The-Moon Marigolds*	Anthony Shaffer *Sleuth*	John Guare *The House of Blue Leaves*	No Award	David Storey *Home*
1972	No Award	David Rabe *Sticks and Bones*	No Award	Jean Genet *The Screens*	Jason Miller *That Championship Season*
1973	Jason Miller *That Championship Season*	Jason Miller *That Champion Season*	Lanford Wilson *The Hot L Baltimore*	No Award	David Storey *The Changing Room*
1974	*No Award*	Joseph A. Walker *The River Niger*	Miguel Pinero *Short Eyes*	No Award	David Storey *The Contractor*
1975	**Edward Albee** *Seascape*	Peter Shaffer *Equus*	Ed Bullins *The Taking of Miss Janie*	No Award	Peter Shaffer *Equus*
1976	Marvin Hamlisch, music Edward Kleban, lyrics Nicholas Dante, book James Kirkwood, book *A Chorus Line*	Tom Stoppard *Travesties*	David Rabe *Streamers*	No Award	Tom Stoppard *Travesties*
1977	Michael Cristofer *The Shadow Box*	Michael Cristofer *The Shadow Box*	David Mamet *American Buffalo*	No Award	Simon Gray *Otherwise Engaged*

	PULITZER PRIZE	TONY AWARD	NY DRAMA CRITICS CIRCLE AWARD		
			Best American	Best Foreign	Best Play
1978	Donald L. Coburn *The Gin Game*	Hugh Leonard *Da*	Hugh Leonard *Da*		
1979	Sam Shepard *Buried Child*	Bernard Pomerance *The Elephant Man*	Bernard Pomerance *The Elephant Man*		
1980	Lanford Wilson *Talley's Folly*	Mark Medoff *Children of a Lesser God*	No Award	Harold Pinter *Betrayal*	Lanford Wilson *Talley's Folly*
1981	Beth Henley *Crimes of the Heart*	Peter Shaffer *Amadeus*	Beth Henley *Crimes of the Heart*	No Award	Athol Fugard *A Lesson from Aloes*
1982	Charles Fuller *A Soldier's Play*	David Edgar *The Life and Adventures of Nicholas Nickleby*	Charles Fuller *A Soldier's Play*	No Award	David Edgar *The Life and Adventures of Nicholas Nickleby*
1983	Marsha Norman *'night, Mother*	Harvey Fierstein *Torch Song Trilogy*	No Award	David Hare *Plenty*	Neil Simon *Brighton Beach Memoirs*
1984	David Mamet *Glengarry Glen Ross*	Tom Stoppard *The Real Thing*	David Mamet *Glengarry Glen Ross*	No Award	Tom Stoppard *The Real Thing*
1985	Stephen Sondheim, music/lyrics James Lapine, book *Sunday in the Park with George*	Neil Simon *Biloxi Blues*	August Wilson *Ma Rainey's Black Bottom*		
1986	No Award	Herb Gardener *I'm Not Rappaport*	Michael Frayn *Benefactors*	No Award	Sam Shepard *A Lie of the Mind*
1987	August Wilson *Fences*	August Wilson *Fences*	No Award	Christopher Hampton *Les Liaisons Dangereuses*	August Wilson *Fences*

	PULITZER PRIZE	TONY AWARD	NY DRAMA CRITICS CIRCLE AWARD		
			Best American	Best Foreign	Best Play
1988	Alfred Uhry *Driving Miss Daisy*	David Henry Hwang *M. Butterfly*	No Award	Athol Fugard *Road to Mecca*	August Wilson *Joe Turner's Come and Gone*
1989	Wendy Wasserstein *The Heidi Chronicles*	Wendy Wasserstein *The Heidi Chronicles*	No Award	Brian Friel *Aristocrats*	Wendy Wasserstein *The Heidi Chronicles*
1990	August Wilson *The Piano Lesson*	Frank Galati *The Grapes of Wrath*	No Award	Peter Nichols *Privates on Parade*	August Wilson *The Piano Lesson*
1991	Neil Simon *Lost in Yonkers*	Neil Simon *Lost in Yonkers*	No Award	Timberlake Wertenbaker *Our Country's Good*	John Guare *Six Degrees of Separation*
1992	Robert Schenkkan *The Kentucky Cycle*	Brian Friel *Dancing at Lughnasa*	August Wilson *Two Trains Running*	No Award	Brian Friel *Dancing at Lughnasa*
1993	Tony Kushner *Angels in America: Millennium Approaches*	Tony Kushner *Angels in America: Millennium Approaches*	No Award	Frank McGuinness *Someone Who'll Watch Over Me*	Tony Kushner *Angels in America: Millennium Approaches*
1994	**Edward Albee** **Three Tall Women**	Tony Kushner *Angels in America: Perestroika*	**Edward Albee** **Three Tall Women**		
1995	Horton Foote *The Young Man from Atlanta*	Terrence McNally *Love! Valour! Compassion!*	Terrence McNally *Love! Valour! Compassion!*	No Award	Tom Stoppard *Arcadia*
1996	Jonathan Larson *Rent*	Terrence McNally *Master Class*	No Award	Brian Friel *Molly Sweeney*	August Wilson *Seven Guitars*
1997	No Award	Alfred Uhry *The Last Night of Ballyhoo*	No Award	David Hare *Skylight*	Paula Vogel *How I Learned to Drive*
1998	Paula Vogel *How I Learned to Drive*	Yasmina Reza *Art*	Tina Howe *Pride's Crossing*	No Award	Yasmina Reza *Art*

	PULITZER PRIZE	TONY AWARD	NY DRAMA CRITICS CIRCLE AWARD		
			Best American	Best Foreign	Best Play
1999	Margaret Edson *Wit*	Warren Leight *Side Man*	No Award	Patrick Marber *Closer*	Margaret Edson *Wit*
2000	Donald Margulies *Dinner with Friends*	Michael Frayn *Copenhagen*	No Award	Michael Frayn *Copenhagen*	August Wilson *Jitney*
2001	David Auburn *Proof*	David Auburn *Proof*	David Auburn *Proof*	No Award	Tom Stoppard *The Invention of Love*
2002	Suzan-Lori Parks *Topdog/Underdog*	**Edward Albee** ***The Goat: or, Who Is Sylvia?***	**Edward Albee** ***The Goat: or, Who Is Sylvia?***		
2003	Nilo Cruz *Anna in the Tropics*	Richard Greenburg *Take Me Out*	No Award	Alan Bennett *Talking Heads*	Richard Greenburg *Take Me Out*
2004	Doug Wright *I Am My Own Wife*	Doug Wright *I Am My Own Wife*	Lynn Nottage *Intimate Apparel*		
2005	John Patrick Shanley *Doubt, a Parable*	John Patrick Shanley *Doubt, a Parable*	No Award	Martin McDonagh *The Pillowman*	John Patrick Shanley *Doubt, a Parable*
2006	No Award	Alan Bennet *The History Boys*	Alan Bennett *The History Boys*		
2007	David Lindsay-Abaire *Rabbit Hole*	Tom Stoppard *The Coast of Utopia*	August Wilson *Radio Gulf*	No Award	Tom Stoppard *The Coast of Utopia*
2008	Tracy Letts *August: Osage County*	Tracy Letts *August: Osage County*	Tracy Letts *August: Osage County*		

INDEX

The entries in the index include highlights from the main In an Hour essay portion of the book.

ABOUT THE AUTHOR

E. Teresa Choate is an Associate Professor and Assistant Chair at the Department of Theatre in the College of Visual and Performing Arts at Kean University in Union, New Jersey. She teaches theater history and dramatic literature, performance theory, dramaturgy, and script analysis, as well as period styles of acting. She is also a director who has mounted over seventy productions to date. She holds an alphabet soup's worth of degrees in theater: PhD (UCLA), MFA in directing (Catholic University of America), MA (Denver University). She is currently the President of Alpha Psi Omega, the National Honor Theatre Society for colleges and universities.

NOTE FROM THE AUTHOR

I would like to thank Prof. Wayne Garrett of the Department of English at David Lipscomb University for his assistance in reviewing and providing feedback on the essay; Cliff Jewell, my husband, for his unconditional support; and Kean University's Department of Theatre faculty, staff, and students for their support and encouragement.

Know the playwright, love the play.

Open a new door to theater study, performance, and audience satisfaction with these Playwrights In an Hour titles.

ANCIENT GREEK

Aeschylus Aristophanes Euripides Sophocles

RENAISSANCE

William Shakespeare

MOD

Antc   812.09 AL1C
Hen
Arth   Choate, E. Teresa, 1953-   rg
       Albee in an hour
Fran   Central Nonfiction CIRC -
Tenn   2nd & 3rd fls
       02/11

CONTEMPORARY

Edward Albee Alan Ayckbourn Samuel Beckett
Theresa Rebeck Sarah Ruhl Sam Shepard Tom Stoppard
August Wilson

To purchase or for more information
visit our web site inanhourbooks.com